‹ *The Book of* ›

BEER PONG

The Official Guide to the Sport of Champions

by BEN APPLEBAUM and DAN DISORBO

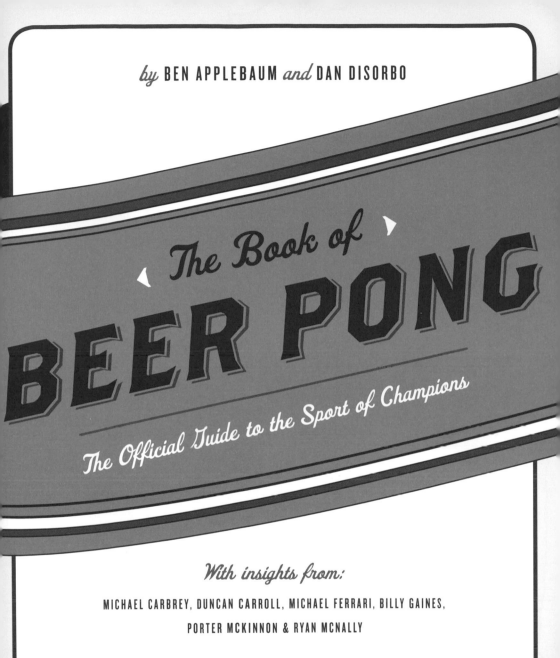

The Book of

BEER PONG

The Official Guide to the Sport of Champions

With insights from:

MICHAEL CARBREY, DUNCAN CARROLL, MICHAEL FERRARI, BILLY GAINES,
PORTER MCKINNON & RYAN MCNALLY

CHRONICLE BOOKS
SAN FRANCISCO

Library of Congress Cataloging-in-Publication Data is available.

ISBN: 978-0-8118-6632-3

Manufactured in China

Designed by Andrew Schapiro
Typeset by DC Type
Typeset in Hoefler, Knockout, and Brothers

10 9 8 7 6 5 4 3 2 1

Chronicle Books LLC
680 Second Street
San Francisco, CA 94107
www.chroniclebooks.com

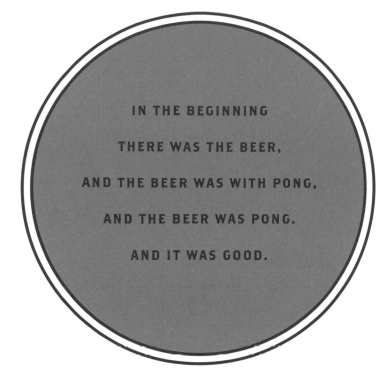

IN THE BEGINNING

THERE WAS THE BEER,

AND THE BEER WAS WITH PONG,

AND THE BEER WAS PONG.

AND IT WAS GOOD.

IMPORTANT NOTICE

Beer Pong is a sport that happens to involve beer, although you are welcome to use any beverage of your choice, even water.

The material contained in this book is presented only for informational purposes. The publisher and authors do not condone or advocate in any way underage drinking or the consumption of large quantities of alcohol, and we accept no liability for the consequences of illegal drinking or overindulgence.

Underage drinking and excessive alcohol consumption are extremely dangerous, and no one should do it. Drink responsibly, know your limits, never drink and drive, and please do not give Beer Pong a bad name.

PLEASE PLAY RESPONSIBLY.

TABLE OF
Awesomeness

Introduction

BEER PONG IS NOT A GAME.

BEER PONG IS A SPORT. It is a sport of champions, where legends are born and heroes are made, one cup at a time. A sport of precision, where inches separate winners from losers. A sport of skill and focus, where excellence comes from exacting form, and greatness comes from unyielding mental fortitude.

For those of you who have somehow managed to remain oblivious to mankind's single greatest achievement, understand that the act of throwing Ping-Pong balls into cups of beer is more than a simple pastime. Imagine the head-to-head intensity of a prizefight, the strategy of a chess match, and the shameless self-congratulation of an NFL touchdown dance. Now mix it with the pressure of a game-winning free throw and the alcohol consumption of a Russian parliamentary meeting. That's Beer Pong, truly an amalgam of the very best of sport—and, one could argue, the very best of humanity.

Beer Pong is also a testament to the natural progression of competition. In pursuit of new ways to prove individual superiority over one's peers, the human race is continuously creating physical contests, from the epic gladiatorial battles in the Colosseum to the professional sports industry of today. Unlike those forms of competition, which have either gone extinct or stagnated, however, Beer Pong is still in the throes of its Darwinian evolution. And we—the players and fans of the sport—have a chance to shape history with our own hands. And elbows.

Because of this responsibility, we've spent hundreds of hours doing in-field research to create this book: the first official guide to the sport of Beer Pong.

There's no denying the fact that Beer Pong has come a long way. What started out as a pastime for Ivy League fraternity brothers has transcended the obscurity of dorm rooms and fraternity houses and established itself as a mainstream sport. It's risen out of dank basements and into popular culture. It's infiltrated bars, tailgates, corporate parties, and even wedding receptions. As it traverses the mainstream and flows toward total and unequivocal global domination, a proper explanation of the details surrounding this sport is in order.

Beer Pong's organic growth has created a mashed-up landscape in which many variations of the sport are played from state to state, town to town, sketchy student apartment to sketchy student apartment. Right now, as Beer Pong reaches its Gladwellian tipping point, it is critical to establish a comprehensive catalog of the sport. Thus we have endeavored to gather the game's greatest minds to establish, for the first time, standardized rules of play.

We're also committed to helping individuals improve their game: to step it up a notch, to take it the next level, and to embrace a wide array of other self-improvement clichés. Competition among Beer Pong players has reached unprecedented levels. And as this trend continues, so does the need to arm oneself with the tools required to survive what could potentially be a disastrous lesson in preparedness.

It's surprising how easily the institution of Beer Pong can find its way into one's life. Ambassadors of the sport are everywhere. From the Beer Pong tales told by friends and family to random personal encounters with Beer Pong tables at parties and bars, the impact of this wonderful pastime is omnipresent. If you are reading this, you obviously have some interest in the details of this sport. Whether you are a seasoned veteran looking to further your already extensive knowledge or an inquisitive parent wondering what your children's college tuition is really buying, this book will provide you with an unprecedented glimpse into the Beer Pong phenomenon.

In this pioneering attempt to catalog and explain the world of Beer Pong, we've not only taken a step toward legitimizing what has been and always will be a controversial activity, but we've also attempted to explain this institution holistically, offering not merely a book of rules and playing tips, but a broad view of the sport's participants, its history, and its future. We've combined our personal expertise along with extensive interviews with industry luminaries to create a resource not just for you, our reader, but for the whole sport. And in doing that, maybe—just maybe—we can help preserve the maverick streak at the very heart of the American spirit.

SO GAME ON, FUTURE CHAMPIONS OF BEER PONG. GAME ON.

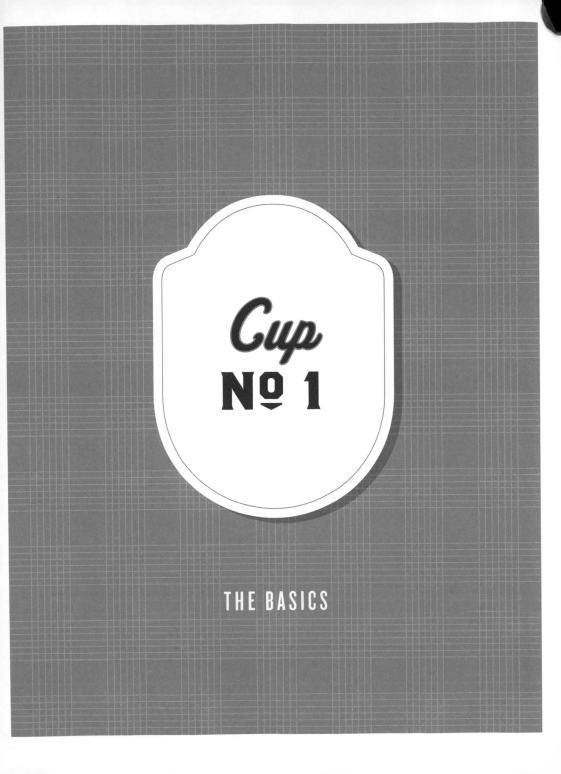

Cup
№ 1

THE BASICS

WELCOME TO THE WONDERFUL WORLD OF BEER PONG.

YOU ARE ABOUT TO EMBARK on a personal journey—a journey into the wonderful world of cups and balls. It will take you through challenges, victories, and even spillage. But most important, it will lead to growth.

Beer Pong encompasses the best of athletics—without the negatives. You still get the thrill of competition, the chance to develop a skill set, the adulation of the crowd—but without the depressing scandals, outrageous ticket prices, and omnipresent corporate sponsors so prevalent in most of today's major sports.

With this in mind, it is time to orient you to the ins, outs, and almost-ins of the sport. This chapter provides an overview of the whats, whys, whos, and whens. And we'll also take a moment to talk about something every Beer Pong enthusiast thinks about: safety.

Naturally, your level of familiarity with this culture will largely determine the usefulness of much of the information to follow. If you fancy yourself a professional, perhaps you should be selective in what you choose to read. If you are a novice, we recommend you pay close attention. But no matter your skill level, you will find the knowledge that follows to be an invaluable foundation for improving your game.

What
IS BEER PONG?

The rules, regulations, and game play will be explained in full detail later. But here we'd like to bring you a quick overview to lay the appropriate foundation for your lifetime of involvement in the sport.

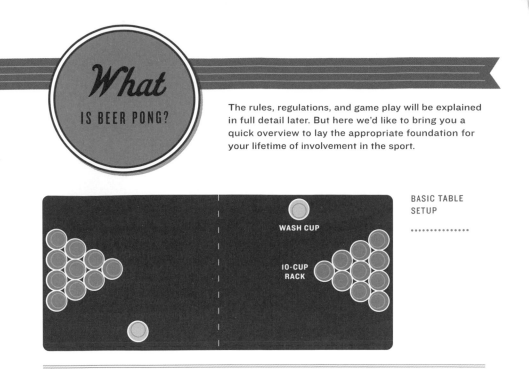

BASIC TABLE SETUP
....

WASH CUP

10-CUP RACK

THE SETUP

Beer Pong is a team sport of skill. There are two 2-player teams, one team on each side of a table, and a number of cups set up on each side. Starting from the back of a table, 10 plastic cups are arranged in a pyramid-shaped "rack" at each end of said table. These cups are filled with a mutually agreed-upon volume of a mutually agreed-upon beverage. Two additional cups of water are furnished for cleaning purposes.

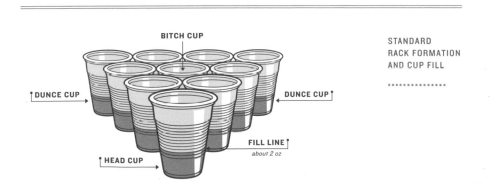

BITCH CUP

DUNCE CUP

DUNCE CUP

FILL LINE
about 2 oz

HEAD CUP

STANDARD RACK FORMATION AND CUP FILL
....

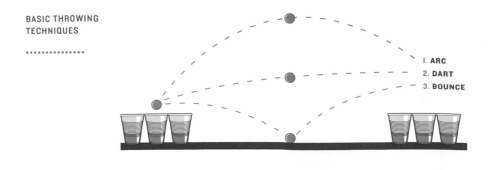

1. ARC
2. DART
3. BOUNCE

GAME PLAY

The two teams stand on opposite sides of the table and attempt to throw, bounce, or otherwise propel a regulation Ping-Pong ball into their opponent's cups on the opposite side of the table. The two teams alternate turns, with each member of the team throwing a single ball on each turn. When their turn is over, the other team throws their two balls.

SCORING

When a player successfully throws a ball into an opponent's cup, the opponent must remove the cup and drink its contents. Empty cups are taken out of play. The first team to eliminate all their opponents' cups wins the game. Simple enough? Of course, as with any sport, there are countless variations and nuances in the rules and game play, which we'll elaborate on later, but for the purpose of this chapter, that's Beer Pong in a nutshell.

COACH SAYS

Keep your rack tight and level and your opponents will do the same.

Why
IT'S SO POPULAR

Now that you know what Beer Pong is, let us examine why it's even worth playing—let alone reading a whole book about. To that end, we've compiled some of the top reasons behind its meteoric rise in popularity.

PURITY

In many ways, Beer Pong is the last true sport; it's still essentially the people's game. It's the only great sport that hasn't been corrupted by big business, inflated salaries, and excessive use of human growth hormones. It's also the only sport left where hopeless underdogs can transform themselves into winners with only a few well-placed throws. And yet, despite Beer Pong's being such a pivotal stone in the temple of society, few know of this great sport's roots. We'll change that in the following chapter.

HUMAN DRAMA

Beer Pong is and always has been a contest of gladiatorial proportions. With dire consequences looming overhead, success rides entirely on one's ability to master a diverse skill set and translate it into a winning effort. The comparisons to ancient Roman combat are obvious: the roaring crowds of spectators, the precise movements, the adrenaline, the enduring of substance- or injury-induced impairment, and the crushing blow of defeat. And the best part is that all of this unfolds in your living room.

ACCESSIBILITY

Beer Pong remains a sport of the people, for the people. No greens fees. No questionably funded stadiums. No expensive equipment. It arose from a culture of limited resources but unlimited ingenuity—that of the American college student. All the equipment can be sourced in your average dorm room. Additionally, the sport doesn't require any freakish physical gifts. Short, tall, skinny, fat, jock, physics major—Beer Pong welcomes all with open arms.

BONDING

Few things unite North Americans more than sports and drinking. The genius of Beer Pong is that it combines both in one compact activity. Thus, it creates the optimal petri dish for the growth and spreading of the organism known as bonding. In one respect, your teammate becomes your copilot, with whom you'll navigate the downs and upchucks of the sport.

GENDER NEUTRALITY

There is a common misconception that Beer Pong is a male-dominated sport. In reality, it provides the battle of the sexes a level—though sometimes beer-soaked—playing field. Men and women compete side by side, as equals. If there are any charges of gender bias, one would only need to point to some of the preferential rules for women (like defensive blowing) to understand that Beer Pong is a sport with a truly glassless ceiling.

ALL-PRO QUOTE

When I first learned of this great sport called Beer Pong, my friend and I would kick ass in whatever game we played in. This gave us the respect of the guys we partied with because they knew that at any point in the game we could potentially beat them. We were the only girl team in the league at the time, but we would always prove ourselves to those we were playing against.

We'd always get that same old routine of, "Oh, we can beat these girls easy." There's nothing better than to sink that last cup and get the look of, "Did that really happen? Did we just get beat by a couple of girls?"

We wound up ranked second-place throughout the season, out of 60-plus teams. So it goes to show that no matter what gender or (legal) age you are, Beer Pong is a great sport.

—AMBER MORALES,
Founder - New Mexico Beer Pong League

AMERICAN-NESS

Charges of xenophobia and nationalistic myopia aside, America kicks ass. But despite our nation's strength, America's relative youth has caused its footprint on the sports world to be more "me too" than "me first." Unfortunately, true homegrown all-American sports are few and far between. Football? This juggernaut is merely a butched-up version of British rugby. Baseball? The beloved national pastime is but a less-boring variation of cricket. NASCAR? While its title as sport is questionable, its late entry into the long-established tradition of auto racing in Europe is not.

ONLY THREE MAJOR AMERICAN SPORTS HAVE ORIGINATED ON DOMESTIC SOIL—BUT WHAT HAS BECOME OF THEM?

1. BASKETBALL. *While birthed in Springfield, Massachusetts, it's now being dominated by players from China, Germany, and, sadly, even France.*

2. LACROSSE. *A Native American invention, it's fast, violent, and huge on college campuses. While that would normally make it perfect, it's missing two critical components: a national following and beer.*

3. BEER PONG. *The ultimate embodiment of American competition. And more than any other sport, it combines the three things we love most:*

▷ ENTERTAINMENT—OVER-THE-TOP SHOWMANSHIP, HYPE, EXCITEMENT

▷ SPORT—COMPETITION, SMACK TALK, WINNER-TAKES-ALL MENTALITY

▷ CONSUMPTION—BUYING STUFF, DRINKING STUFF, BUYING MORE STUFF TO DRINK

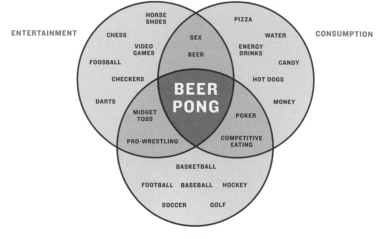

Whom
TO PLAY WITH

The essence of Beer Pong is the tension between teamwork and competition. So, as part of our overview of the sport, we'll look at the interpersonal dynamics of the game and provide some advice on maximizing your success.

WHAT TO LOOK FOR IN A TEAMMATE

Unlike boxing, marathon running, and professional basketball, Beer Pong is not an individual sport. But unlike other team sports, in which you can have anywhere from 5 to 12 players on a team, in Beer Pong you have a squad of only two. The "team" is thus a much more concentrated and intense unit, and finding the right playing partner becomes critical.

ALL-PRO QUOTE

It's a two-man team, and you are only as good as your partner so you have to learn their strengths and weaknesses and form a good game plan to be successful.

—MICHAEL POPIELARSKI
2009 World Series of Beer Pong Champion & 7-time World Beer Pong Tour Champion

IN CHOOSING A TEAMMATE, LOOK FOR THE FOLLOWING IMPORTANT ATTRIBUTES.

DEPENDABILITY. *On a two-person team, there's no room for a slacker. Even if they don't hit as many cups as you, you need someone who will carry their own weight—and yours, when you are off.*

FOCUS. *This is not a sport for the scatterbrained. Make sure your potential teammate can follow a train of thought and is at least in the ballpark when asked, "How many fingers am I holding up?"*

PEOPLE YOU COULD ASK TO BE YOUR TEAMMATE:

··················

- ▷ Significant other
- ▷ Classmate
- ▷ Fellow fraternity/sorority member
- ▷ Cool sibling
- ▷ Stepparent you call by their first name
- ▷ Roommate

PEOPLE YOU SHOULD NOT ASK TO BE YOUR TEAMMATE:

··················

- ▷ Cop
- ▷ Professor
- ▷ Nun
- ▷ In-law
- ▷ Uncool sibling
- ▷ Cellmate
- ▷ Roommate

COMMITMENT. *Lesser sports may accept quitters. But not this one. You need to make sure your teammate is with you through thick and thin. Don't settle for anything less than Oprah-like devotion.*

BEER PONG SKILLS. *When looking to win Beer Pong games, it's best to look for someone who possesses a certain intangible quality known as the ability to win Beer Pong games. This advice alone justifies the price of this book.*

ALL-PRO QUOTE

I think teamwork is undeniably important. You have to have confidence in your partner, or it begins to affect your game. If I know my partner is hitting, I feed off of that. If I know he is off, I need to do a little more. I think ability has very little to do with teamwork, and more with how you play together.

—NICHOLAS VELISSARIS,
2006 World Series of Beer Pong Champion

What

TO EXPECT FROM THE COMPETITION

Unless you are running your own tournament, you cannot control whom you'll be playing against. To help you prepare, we've studied hundreds of games and determined the eight archetypal players you're most likely to face.

THE RULE NAZI, AKA CAPTAIN RULEBOOK, THE BYLAW BANDIT, DIRK STICKLER

This player takes the game way too seriously. And that's coming from the people who wrote a whole book on it. Sure, this type helps maintain the legitimacy of the sport. But playing him is not going to be fun.

VERDICT: *Beating him will be tough, but very, very satisfying.*

THE BEGINNER, AKA BEER PONG VIRGIN, THAT HOME-SCHOOLED KID, FISH

They need handholding and babysitting. Their naivety about the sport is charming at first—until they reflexively catch your would-be winning shot.

VERDICT: *Watch out for beginner's luck—but don't worry, it won't last long.*

THE HOTTIE, AKA THE HOT CHICK, TROUBLE

This player brings talent of a different sort—a sexy, glandular sort. She has a tendency to dress provocatively and apply makeup both before and during the game. Not all female players fall into this category, mind you. Just those who compete on looks.

VERDICT: *Fight the distraction factor, think about cold weather, and make the shots.*

THE DAD, AKA OLD MAN, THE NARC

He stands out like a sore, balding, old thumb. No one knows how or why he's playing. But, numbed by life experiences, he possesses superior focus. And since he doesn't understand half your insults, smack talk is ineffective.

VERDICT: *Remind him that it's past his bedtime, and he'll start choking.*

THE DRINKER, AKA FLOUNDER, FARLEY, LOHAN

This player is just here for the party—playing the game comes a distant second. Since he's looking for any reason to a chug-a-lug, he literally can't lose.

VERDICT: *Give him what he wants, a good old-fashioned beat-down.*

THE RINGER, AKA THE HUSTLER, RAINMAN, MINNESOTA SPLATS

The most dangerous type of player to go against. She'll lull you into a false sense of superiority before cleaning your proverbial clock. Ringers come in all shapes and sizes—usually the opposite of what you'd expect.

VERDICT: *They win. Sorry, that's the truth.*

BEER PONG FACTOID

In Australia, a ringer is a highly skilled sheep shearer. That's a fact, look it up.

THAT GUY/GIRL, AKA TURD FERGUSON, SLOPPY McGEE

With one too many games under his belt, this player has no self-censor, and loss of faculties is imminent. Beware of potential face-plants on the table.

VERDICT: *Wave off this game. Get him a cab and a Handi Wipe—then send him home.*

THE MOUTH, AKA MR. FRATASTIC, SELF-APPOINTED WORLD CHAMPION

Thinks he's God's gift to the game—and wants you to bask in his greatness. This player talks smack endlessly and uses his yearly quotient of the word "bro" in the first five minutes of play.

VERDICT: *Read this book and, for the love of everyone, beat his ass.*

When

TO PLAY

There are countless situations where the playing of Beer Pong is not only fitting, but actually achieves a higher social purpose. Below is a list of appropriate times to play. This is by no means exhaustive. The only limits are your imagination, and perhaps the law.

THE PREGAME GAME

This occasion is but a means to an end. And that end could be anything from a night out on the town to a full-fledged, out-of-control house party. In this capacity, Beer Pong serves as a social appetizer before the main course. While wins and losses aren't critical, they can provide a topic of conversation for the night ahead.

THE POSTGAME GAME

This game starts after everyone returns from a long night on the town. For some reason, the participants feel that 3 a.m. is the perfect time to set up the table and start playing. While fun in the moment, this game is rarely remembered and often broken up by the cops due to its lack of popularity with neighbors.

THE ICEBREAKER GAME

Thanks to its universality, a game of Beer Pong provides the perfect catalyst for cementing new bonds. Although it is not a formal part of orientation, any college student can attest to the powers of a few well-intentioned games for establishing rapport and camaraderie between strangers.

THE STATEMENT GAME

Sometimes the act of playing is an act of defiance—an affable rebellion against societal norms. While playing a game at your wedding reception or during a corporate retreat is fun, most of the enjoyment comes after the fact, when you tell everyone what you did.

••••••••••••••••

To avoid damaging the fragile reputation of this fledging sport, refrain
from playing at the following times:

▷ Alcoholics Anonymous
   meetings
▷ Non-Irish funerals
▷ Birthday parties for children
   under 21
▷ Anytime during the birth
   process
▷ Most religious services

THE MARATHON GAME

This is about quantity, not quality. As the game goes on into the wee hours of the morn, all bets are off. These debacles are usually characterized by a number of teams randomly signing up, with only a few actually being any good. The inevitable—and often lopsided—result is an amusing spectacle of trash-talking, nudity, and overall good times.

THE TOURNAMENT GAME

These formalized events are dedicated to an appreciation of the sport—and to the cold hard cash at stake. This is a serious game played by serious players who somehow manage to have a good time, too. See Cup #8 for more information on hosting your own event.

ALL-PRO QUOTE

Beer pong has become way more than a party game. It's a high-level competitive sport that involves consistency, strategy, and a specific game plan.

—MICHAEL POPIELARSKI
2009 World Series of Beer Pong Champion & 7-time World Beer Pong Tour Champion

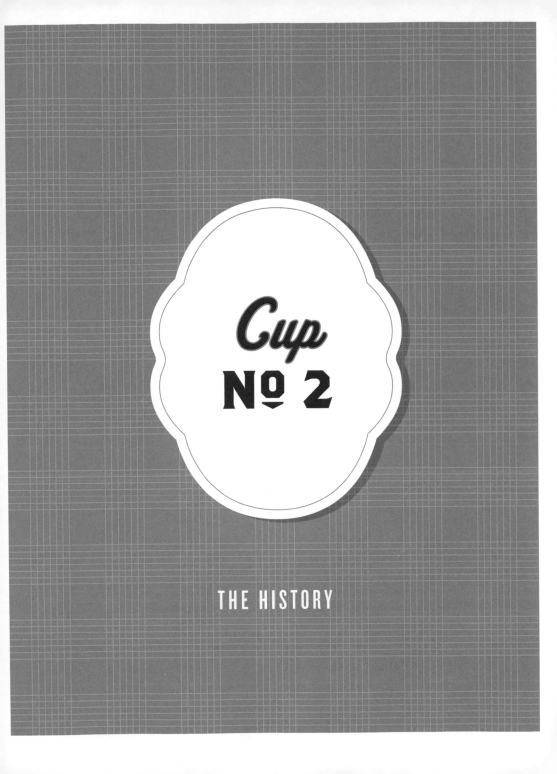

Cup
№ 2

THE HISTORY

THEY SAY, "TO GET WHERE YOU ARE GOING, KNOW WHERE YOU ARE FROM."

NOWHERE IS THIS MORE TRUE than in our own fair sport. In order for Beer Pong to realize its full potential and attain the praise it so deserves, we must first recognize those who threw balls before us.

All sports have their founding fathers, from basketball's Dr. James Naismith to baseball's Abner Doubleday. And all sports celebrate their great innovators—think of Fosbury's flop, Kareem's sky hook, and Ickey's shuffle. Beer Pong is no different. But why does its rich and storied history remain shrouded in mystery? How can its revolutionaries remain so unbronzed?

It may be because the sport's growth has been so organic and unintentional. Or maybe because it has been so connected to a population not known for factual accuracy: college students. In any event, the following chapter is our attempt to lay the foundation for appreciation, attribution, and further study of this sport's history—and ultimately, its future.

Since Beer Pong is so perfect yet so complex, many people assume that it must have been intelligently designed by a higher power—willed into existence without peer or predecessor. But if one were to look into the genome of Beer Pong, one might be surprised (or possibly heartbroken) to find traces of influence from other sports of the past millennium.

BEER PONG'S
Ancestors

While many of these sports have become extinct or faded into the background, they each contributed something, however small, to the creation and evolution of Beer Pong.

CIRCA 500 BC—KOTTABOS

The greatest invention of ancient Greece: the first drinking game. In its simplest form, it was played by flinging wine out of a cup while calling out the name of the player's beloved (an early form of the shout-out). The objective would be to land the flying booze onto a circular, disc-like ornament.

1300 AD—SKITTLES

A sport similar to bowling, skittles involved throwing an object (anything from a baton to a rock to a lump of cheese) into nine pins, or "skittles." All the rage in medieval Europe, and still played today in some circles, it clearly taps into the same sporting vein as Beer Pong.

1400 AD—TABLE SHUFFLEBOARD

Demanding a mastery of distance and discipline, table shuffle-board requires players to slide pucks across a table, attempting to land them in a determined scoring area, while also knocking their opponent's pucks out of said area. The triangular forma-tion at the end of a long table would later become an even more familiar sight.

1700 AD—THE PUZZLE JUG

The French created this game solely to be played in taverns and at parties. The jug is a piece of pottery molded with a number of holes and perforations. The player had to plug the correct holes before drinking or else go home with a shirt stained in wine. This brought a modicum of sophistication to the drinking game.

1880 AD—PING-PONG

Beer Pong's sober cousin was first played as an after-dinner amusement by upper-class Victorians as a way to mimic the new outdoor sport of tennis. Later it gained popularity among athletes around the world and—thankfully for the sake of Beer Pong—American college students. Today it is the third-most-popular racquet sport. But only the second-most-awesome sport with "pong" in the name.

1891 AD—BASKETBALL

At first glance, this might not appear to be in the Beer Pong family tree, given that it involves running, jumping, and other movements not required in our sport. But the sport did give us the free throw, which interestingly, until 1923, was shot by a specialist—not the fouled player.

1900 AD—GOLDFISH PONG

Thank the carnies for this ultimate gateway game to Beer Pong. All the basics are here: Ping-Pong balls, cups, fluids, and the challenge of accurate tossing. But possibly most important, Goldfish Pong teaches the fundamental life principle that the spoils of victory go to those who can throw a ball into a cup.

BEER PONG FACTOID

The original Ping-Pong ball was a rounded Champagne cork. Keep that in mind next time you are out of balls.

Throwing Stuff at Things:
THE PRECISION SPORT FAMILY

As we proclaimed in the introduction—those first few pages that no one read—Beer Pong is not a drinking game. In fact, it belongs to a long tradition of precision sports. Golf, darts, billiards, and archery are perhaps the most common and mainstream variants. But the proud tradition of throwing stuff at things comes in many variations

HORSESHOES
A form of the game was played by the ancient Greeks, and it is still played today by ancient Greeks, Italians, and Poles.

BOCCE
The sport dates back to the Roman Empire, but the idea of throwing a ball at a target, preferably with drinks nearby, remains popular to this day.

TEJO
This traditional Colombian sport involves throwing a metallic plate to hit a mound of *mechas* (gunpowder!)—making it almost as cool as Beer Pong.

WASHER PITCHING
Throwing a washer at a target was a popular form of pre–Beer Pong entertainment for generations of Midwesterners. The English have versions called toad in the hole (played with disks) and pitch penny (played with coins).

SKEE-BALL
Invented in Philadelphia in 1909, it was first considered gambling, which explains its addictive properties to ticket-hungry 12-year-olds.

BEER PONG'S
Genesis

The previous section examined the sporting influences that provided the rich, fertile soil for the growth of modern-day Beer Pong; now it is time to see exactly how and where the sport germinated, took root, and began reaching toward the heavens.

Many of the details of its origins are debatable and—surprising for a sport that involves beer—fuzzy. Here, we present some of the most compelling theories.

THE BIRTH OF A MOVEMENT: THE DARTMOUTH BANG THEORY

In rural New Hampshire resides an institution of incalculable esteem and notoriety: Dartmouth College. Its reputation is undoubtedly bolstered by Ivy League academics, renowned alumni like Robert Frost, and of course its cinematic claim to fame as the inspiration for *Animal House*. But these are mere résumé fillers compared to the school's most significant contribution to the world: the invention of an early game that somewhat resembles modern-day Beer Pong.

Jere Daniell, Dartmouth College's valedictorian for the class of 1955 and a retired history professor at the school, remembers how a friendly basement game of Ping-Pong turned into much more. "It wasn't uncommon for us to be playing a game of Ping-Pong before someone changed things up and put a paper cup of beer on the table," recalled Daniell. "We used to have fun. We would try to knock over the other guy's cup, and if you did, he'd have to chug his beer."

While a misplaced cup during a table tennis game in the 1950s was the spark for the birth of Beer Pong, it took more than a decade for the fire of Beer Pong to ignite. An article in the *Dartmouth Independent* [Oct. 2007] provides insight into this sluggish start. One reason for it was that the college was still an all-male institution. Thus, crucial hours that could have been spent playing Beer Pong were wasted on road trips to Mt. Holyoke College, a nearby women's college.

Thus, it remained a casual pastime. "We never had all these rules," remembers Daniell. "We were just playing Ping-Pong with beer. Now it seems like there's a lot of organization and regulation that goes into these games, which is something that we never had."

This would all change, though, in 1972, when the admittance of women to Dartmouth fanned the sport's flames—not just through the benefits of their proximity, but as players in their own right. Another factor in the sport's popularity surge was the new availability of an advanced piece of equipment: cheap plastic cups, which allowed for more-forgiving bounces and easier cleanup.

The sport was now fully stoked, and according to the *Dartmouth Independent* article, Beer Pong was even briefly recognized as an official intramural sport—the nation's first college-sponsored sport that involved beer. But in 1977 the college brass "de-recognized" the sport—driving it back underground, literally, into the basements of various campus fraternities. This caused a splintering of the rules and game play—a phenomenon that repeated itself when modern-day Beer Pong spread on a national scale.

But despite challenges to the sport by the school administration, by the 1980s the Dartmouth version of Beer Pong was being played on campuses across the Northeast, including Bowdoin, Bucknell, Harvard, Lehigh, Princeton, and Williams.

A BRIEF TAXONOMY OF DARTMOUTH PONG

••••••••••••••••

HOUSE PONG: The earliest, primordial version, which bears the closest resemblance to non-drinking Ping-Pong.

LOB PONG: In this, the most-popular variant, teammates alternate volleys with high, arcing shots, after single bounces on each side. Considered more conversational and leisurely than modern Beer Pong.

SLAM PONG: As in volleyball, one teammate acts as the "server," setting up a vertical shot for the "slammer," who does what the name implies. Compared to Lob Pong, it is much more competitive, and seemingly more popular with alumni.

THE GREAT OPTIMIZATION: THE LEHIGH LEGEND AND THE PADDLE SHATTER OF THE 1980s

Make no mistake about it: Dartmouth Pong is considered by many to be the closest direct ancestor to Beer Pong, as the chimpanzee is to man.

But, while thoroughly entertaining and effective as a social lubricant, Dartmouth Pong lacked what marketing gurus call "viralocity-ness"—in other words, it didn't spread easily. It had several innate limitations: It required Ping-Pong paddles (just two more things for a college student to lose), it employed a full-size table-tennis table (hard to smuggle into dorms), and it was played at a leisurely, rhythmic pace (a poor fit with the high energy of modern college parties).

However, these challenges were overcome by a great optimization of the game that took place in the 1980s. And while some of the details and attributions are still debated, the fact that Beer Pong was taken to the next level is not.

The most popular theory surrounding Beer Pong's creation goes back to a night in the mid-1980s, when the U.S. was captivated by foreign wars—and the college students who didn't take to protesting took to partying. During that time, Lehigh's chapter of the Theta Delta Chi fraternity was partaking in one of its favorite activities: Dartmouth Pong. In the beer-soaked basement of the fraternity house, the brothers waged war by smacking balls toward one another. And during a particularly furious game, something unexpected happened—the Ping-Pong paddles broke. Both of them.

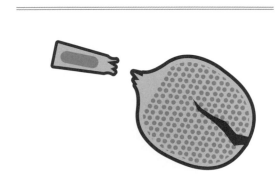

Without paddles, the boys of Theta Delta Chi were left with precious few options. According to the legend, the players decided to continue a particularly competitive game of Dartmouth Pong paddle-less, by hurling the balls into the cups free-throw style. The game was good—real good.

Around that time—and on the other side of the world—a

cease-fire between Israel and the PLO was broken by a Hezbollah suicide bomber's deadly attack on the American barracks in Beirut. This tragedy provided the morbid inspiration for naming this new version of Beer Pong. The president of Theta Delta Chi in 1985 has been quoted as saying: "The game got its name based on an analogy between Ping-Pong balls flying across the table . . . and an idea that the U.S. should bomb Beirut."

And just like that, a game named Beirut was created and the history of sport was forever changed.

BEER PONG FACTOIDS

The first disposable cup was invented by Lawrence Luellen and Hugh Moore in 1907.

COMPETING CREATION THEORIES

••••••••••••••••

While the Lehigh University legend is far and away the most popular of the sport's creation myths, there are other versions in circulation.

THE BUCKNELL BASH HYPOTHESIS: A member of Lehigh's Theta Delta Chi house has admitted to the press that he first witnessed a rudimentary version of paddle-less Dartmouth Pong on a 1983 road trip to nearby Bucknell University. He merely adapted and refined it.

THE SIGMA NU PROPOSITION: Brothers of Sigma Nu at Lehigh claim to have developed the game in 1986 during a particularly rowdy game, which saw all the paddles accidentally destroyed. This postulation may point to an example of convergent cultural evolution—or a rare case of inter-fraternal one-upmanship.

THE SCIENTOLOGIST ASSERTION: 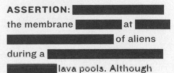 the membrane ███████ at ██████ ███████████████ of aliens during a ████████████████ ████████lava pools. Although Church officials have asked us not to print those details.

THE *Spread* OF BEER PONG

Regardless of its origins, this revised version of Beer Pong was perfectly suited for social diffusion. And socially diffuse it did—from campus to campus, from state to state, from sea to shining sea.

In its latest form, Beer Pong was now new, improved and perfectly designed for greatness. It was fast, so more people could play in a night, it required little special equipment, and it was highly competitive, which inspired word of mouth. Within 10 short years of the Great Optimization of the mid-'80s, modern Beer Pong spread from the fertile crescent of the Lehigh Valley of Pennsylvania to all corners of the country. But how? Following are three possible explanations.

ROAD TRIPS

The late '80s and early '90s featured a confluence of cultural factors—more college students with cars, cheap gas—that aided campus-to-campus diffusion of the game.

THE FRATERNITY-WIRE TRANSMISSION

Many Greek organizations have annual conclaves and meetings where members come together and share everything from bylaws and philosophies to cheat sheets and pledge-education tips. When these conclaves adjourned for the day, it would have been the perfect opportunity to share other traditions. Like Beer Pong.

WINTER/SUMMER BREAK EXCHANGES

When school lets out for break after a long semester, students return home, reconnect with old friends, and share war stories. Eager to brag about hookups and show off newly acquired party traditions, these get-togethers would have presented perfect occasions for introducing the sport to neophytes.

Beer Pong 2.0

No matter the circuitous path it took, Beer Pong arrived. And just in time to thoroughly pervade all of American culture.

Welcome to Beer Pong 2.0.—the next generation of the sport. What was once relegated to the basements of fraternity houses is now being played on the permanently sunny banks of the mainstream. Players of all walks of life have embraced the sport. And its unique form of table-top drama is being played out in backyards, kitchens and wedding receptions across this great land of ours.

The new millennium has witnessed the birth of an entrepreneur movement, which has garnered major media exposure and generated millions of dollars in revenue for American small businesses. And in the process, stoked the fire behind the sport—taking it to new levels.

2004

BOMBED Beer Pong (Full disclosure: That's us.) pioneered the entrepreneur movement by developing the first product line dedicated to the sport. Retailers across America began carrying the popular kit for home games, introducing thousands of adults to the sport. This in turn led to Beer Pong posters, shirts, portable tables and even that great American icon, the Zippo Lighter.

2005

Major beer producer Anheuser-Busch bowed to the popularity of the sport, attempting to forge its own brand known as "Bud Pong."

2006

The first international Beer Pong competition was born, the World Series of Beer Pong. (More on this in Cup #8.)

2008

The first Beer Pong video game was unveiled for the Nintendo Wii to help players hone their real-world skills. While Connecticut Attorney General Dick Blumenthal demanded that the game's name be changed to Pong Toss, its inspiration remains clear.

PRESENT

You are reading *The Book of Beer Pong* written by the good folks at GetBombed.com and CollegeStories.com.

As you can see, Beer Pong has now established itself firmly in our culture. Feature stories have been seen in the *New York Times*, the *Wall Street Journal*, and *Time* magazine. Beer Pong has been the topic of numerous films and television shows, appearing in the cinematic classic *Beer Fest* and reality television's *Big Brother*, for example. Celebrities of all stripes have been seen playing the sport, including politicians looking for the youth vote, Miss America contestants, NBA and NFL stars, '80s sitcom stars, and, regrettably, former boy-band members.

BOTTOM LINE: **BEER PONG MAY HAVE BEEN CREATED IN A COLLEGE BASEMENT SOMEWHERE, BUT NOW IT'S USING THE WHOLE COUNTRY AS ITS TABLE.**

ALL-PRO QUOTE

Beer Pong, when it started out, was just an underground thing, people played in their basements and everything, kind of like *Fight Club*—they just started fighting in the basement. What we're trying to do, just like they tried to do in *Fight Club*, is bring it out of the basement, put it into the spotlight.

—AUSTIN LANHAM,
Cofounder, MD Beer Pong

What's in a Name?

What is the correct name for the sport? Beer Pong or Beirut? The debate over the nomenclature is seen by some as a harmless bar argument, like "pop" versus "soda" or "hoagie" versus "grinder." But this bifurcation is hindering the mainstream acceptance and inevitable global domination of the sport. So all of us in the sport community must get off the metaphorical fence and land on one side of the name debate. As you can assume from the name of our book and the preceding pages, we are strong proponents of Beer Pong. But rather than cram our opinion down your throat, we will present a fair and balanced view of both sides of the argument.

	BEER PONG	BEIRUT
CREDIBILITY	Strong. Dates back to early version of sport at Dartmouth. (1950)	Equally strong. Dates back to current form from Lehigh. (1980)
ETYMOLOGY	A compound word formed from Ping-Pong and beer.	A metaphorical allusion to a geopolitical event involving Middle Eastern factional fighting.
CLARITY OF USAGE	Confuses only Dartmouth students who still play their ancient paddle form.	Confuses only adults and home-schooled poli-sci majors.
SEMANTICS	Has "beer" in title	Too hard to spell
RHYMES WITH	song, bong, dong	root, toot, shoot
POPULARITY*	87% of players prefer	11% of players prefer

VERDICT: FROM HENCEFORTH IT SHALL BE KNOWN AS BEER PONG AND BEER PONG ONLY. AMEN. (UNLESS YOU ARE STUBBORN AND STILL WANT TO CALL IT BEIRUT.)

* GETBOMBED.COM SURVEY

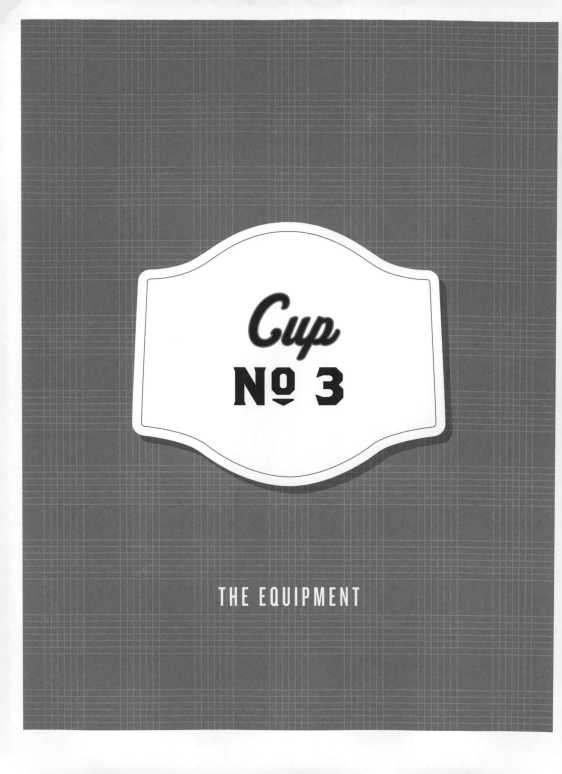

Cup

№ 3

THE EQUIPMENT

OUR JOURNEY TOWARD BEER PONG MASTERY HAS JUST BEGUN.

BUT IT IS HIGH TIME WE EXPLORE some of the more technical aspects of actual game play. Let us begin by detailing the equipment required to partake in this sport.

Despite the high level of skill often demonstrated during a Beer Pong match, very little preparation is actually required to set the stage. Among this sport's many commendable qualities is the fact that it demands minimal, easily accessible, and relatively inexpensive equipment. To get a game going, one need only acquire Ping-Pong balls, cups, a flat surface, and a given volume of potable liquid. Yet this seemingly simple setup can become much more complicated when you consider all your potential choices. What type and size ball is best? Which of the many varieties of cups is ideal? Is there a standard size for a table? And perhaps most important, what liquid is best to play Beer Pong with?

But you need not be concerned. We will not only explain Beer Pong equipment but also provide in-depth instruction on how to build your own table and find suitable substitutes in the event you find yourself unable to acquire a particular piece of gear. And as we've done thus far, we'll also provided a few visual aids for clarification.

Standard EQUIPMENT

Every sport involves basic immutable objects that must be present for competition to take place. Fortunately, the immutable objects of Beer Pong are cheap and plentiful. But don't let that distract you from a proper analysis of the optimal standard equipment.

THE BALL

It takes balls to play this sport—seamless, celluloid table-tennis balls, to be exact. While much has changed since the game diverged from its roots in Ping-Pong, the ball serves as a vestigial reminder of the sport's roots.

The ball is made of high-bouncing, gas-filled celluloid. Celluloid was discovered by Alexander Parks in 1856. After making the discovery, Park described the material as a "hard, horny elastic and waterproof substance," perfect for Beer Pong. However, it wasn't until 1901 when an Englishman, James Gibb, introduced the ball as we know it today after discovering novelty celluloid balls on a trip to the United States.

The optimal size is 40 millimeters in diameter and 2.7 grams in weight. The other specifications are straightforward: The ball should be clean and round, and it should bounce up to approximately 23.3 centimeters when dropped from a height of 30 centimeters. The 40-millimeter ball made an auspicious debut at the table tennis events of the 2000 Olympic Games. It was a controversial attempt to slow down the sport for reasons of commercial viability. While table-tennis professionals still debate the size, Beer Pong enthusiasts are in universal agreement that the new, larger ball is superior to the old 38-millimeter ball, improving control and reducing spin.

BEER PONG FACTOID

Celluloid is easily decomposable, highly flammable, and used in guitar picks as well as Beer Pong balls. Thus, it is a triple threat on the awesomeness scale.

Balls come in a variety of colors, with the most common being white and orange. Many experts prefer orange for the increased visual contrast against white walls and cup interiors. The fact that they do not show the detritus picked up from being dropped on the floor is an added benefit.

Finally, the question remains: How many balls do you need to bring to a game? While the minimum required is two, our experience has proven that you should have at least four for an indoor game, and at least six for playing outdoors. There are few things worse than ending a game due to lost projectiles.

EMERGENCY OPTIONS WHEN A BALL IS NOT AVAILABLE

······················

- ▷ Bottle cap
- ▷ Crumpled-up paper
- ▷ Balled-up duct tape
- ▷ Whittled-down wine cork
- ▷ The "widget" inside a can of Guinness Draught
- ▷ Jawbreaker (may dissolve during game play)

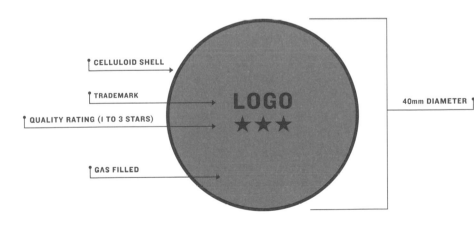

CELLULOID SHELL

TRADEMARK

QUALITY RATING (I TO 3 STARS)

GAS FILLED

LOGO
★ ★ ★

40mm DIAMETER

How to Fix a Dented Ball

WATER METHOD

STEP 1. Bring a pot of water to a rolling boil on a stove or illegal dorm-room hot pot.

STEP 2. Place ball in water for approximately 13 seconds, until dent pops out. Multiple balls can be done simultaneously.

STEP 3. Remove ball with slotted spoon.

STEP 4. Let cool.

STEP 5. Continue your game.

FLAME METHOD

STEP 1. Locate an open flame—preferably a lighter.

STEP 2. Hold ball two to four inches above the flame, moving it around until dent pops out. Do not let fire rest too long in one spot or the ball will melt.

STEP 3. Let cool.

STEP 4. Continue your game.

PAPER METHOD

STEP 1. Find a retailer that sells balls.

STEP 2. Hand over a few dollars for a new set.

STEP 3. Continue your game.

THE CUPS

In Beer Pong, the cups hold more than just fluid—they hold the very meaning of the game. What would basketball be without the basket? What would golf be without the hole? The answer: Not a sport anyone would want to play. Same with Beer Pong. So understandably, selecting the right cup from the sea of options is critical.

MATERIAL

Paper and Styrofoam cups lack the structure to hold up when hit by a ball, and glass and hard plastic washable cups are way too rigid to allow for any ball play. Plus, balls would be dinging and flying everywhere if you were to play with a rack made of glass cups.

Plastic disposable cups offer the best of both worlds. They are strong yet have some give when a ball hits the back rim. A good cup should be made from polypropylene, which is strong, has good chemical resistance, optical clarity, and low moisture/vapor transmission, and is resistant to flavor and odor transfer. All very important features in a piece of equipment that you shoot a ball into and then drink from.

BEER PONG FACTOIDS

Disposable cups are recyclable and washable, so consider reusing them—after a good cleaning, of course. Reduces waste in landfills as well as unnecessary cup runs to the store.

Most disposable plastic cups have a series of ridges on the outside, which not only add strength to the side walls but also give a good grip.

SIZE

While the industry sizes cups based on volume, the most significant dimensions from a Beer Pong standpoint are rim diameter and height. Cups with a rim width of 3⅝ inches and a height of 4⅝ inches are ideal. These dimensions are most common in 16-ounce cups.

EMERGENCY OPTIONS WHEN CUPS ARE NOT AVAILABLE

·················

▷ Coffee cups
▷ Opened and washed soup cans
▷ Beer cans cut in half
▷ Hollowed-out coconuts (if stranded on island)

The smaller 12-ounce and 14-ounce cups offer small rims—and harder shots. The larger 18-ounce versions make it simply too easy. Thus, the 16-ounce cup remains the appropriate compromise.

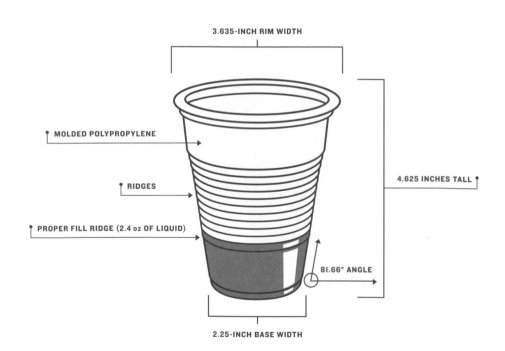

3.635-INCH RIM WIDTH

MOLDED POLYPROPYLENE

RIDGES

PROPER FILL RIDGE (2.4 oz OF LIQUID)

4.625 INCHES TALL

81.66° ANGLE

2.25-INCH BASE WIDTH

The Cup Color Conundrum

While they're not as fiercely contentious as partisans in the "Beer Pong vs. Beirut" and "Bounce vs. No Bounce" debates, there are two divided camps when it comes to the question of cup color. Here we present both sides of the debate.

THE RED PLASTIC CUP

Introduced by the Solo Cup Co. in the 1970s, the red plastic cup was used initially for refreshments such as iced tea and lemonade. But soon college students adopted it as a cheap way to serve—and more important, conceal—beer. It quickly spilled into the mainstream, appearing in movies, TV shows, and countless Facebook photos as the universal sign of "beer party."

Thus, discretion is no longer one of the benefits of the red plastic cup. But for recreational games of Beer Pong, this cup's retail ubiquity is still a big advantage. On the other hand, when used with a white ball, this cup's white interior does not provide enough visual contrast.

 VERDICT: HEAVY ON SYMBOLISM BUT LOW ON FEATURES, THIS CLASSIC CHALICE OF IMBIBING IS STILL SUITABLE FOR A BACKYARD BEER PONG GAME.

THE TRANSPARENT PLASTIC CUP

Clear polypropylene was once relegated to smaller containers destined for an unfortunate fate in doctors' offices. But today, it is put to use in a most-admirable form: the 16-ounce Beer Pong cup.

The most obvious advantage is visibility. The liquid lines can be quickly compared for consistency—preventing any unnecessary disagreements. In terms of game play, these cups provide the greatest and quickest COBE (Confirmation of Ball Entry), which improves the experience of both players and spectators.

 VERDICT: THE TRANSPARENT CUP IS CLEARLY THE BEST CHOICE FOR THE SERIOUS PLAYER.

HOW TO PRACTICE SAFE PONG

....

- ▷ Don't drink from the cups in play—consolidate all beers into a personal drinking cup (called the chill cup).
- ▷ Don't stack empty cups—this just helps transmit funk.
- ▷ Keep several spare balls handy and replace any that are particularly dirty.
- ▷ Wash your balls between games with soap and water.
- ▷ Keep a towel handy to wipe down spills and extremely dirty balls.
- ▷ Consider changing the water in the wash cup between each game.
- ▷ Better yet, make an antimicrobial cocktail for the wash cup with a solution of 60 percent vodka and 40 percent water.
- ▷ Don't lose.
- ▷ Get tested regularly.

Aaron Heffner and Ben Morrissey of George Washington University conducted a study of the microbes present at a typical college Beer Pong game. They found high levels of a bacterial family that contains such species as E. coli, pneumonia, and salmonella—all biological party fouls to be sure. And the worst offender: the wash cup. "The wet and dirty environment serves as a perfect breeding ground, one that supports much growth," says Heffner.

THE WASH CUP

While not directly involved in game play, the wash cup is one of Beer Pong's most unique contributions to the world of sport. Etiquette—and hygiene—dictate that two cups be left on the table, but out of play, for the express purpose of ball washing. Traditionally, these cups are filled with warm tap water.

Throughout the course of a game, the ball will undoubtedly make contact with the floor, an unsanitary table surface, the lip of a recently sipped cup, the lip of a player, and so on. It is believed that a quick rinse in the cup will lessen the transmission of what scientists call "funk."

Interestingly, the player is washing the ball for his opponent's benefit—not his own. This intrinsic selflessness is such an essential part of the game that few players or observers fully appreciate it.

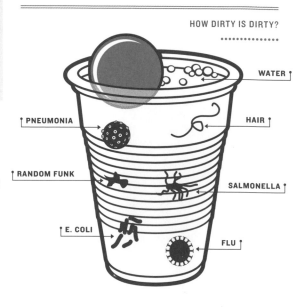

HOW DIRTY IS DIRTY?

....

WATER ↑

↑ PNEUMONIA

HAIR ↑

↑ RANDOM FUNK

SALMONELLA ↑

↑ E. COLI

FLU ↑

THE LIQUID

Although "beer" is in its name, Beer Pong can be played with any potable liquid. But for those fortunate enough to be of legal drinking age—and responsible enough to handle their business—beer is the drink of choice when playing.

Few sports have the luck to feature a component as singular as beer. As the world's oldest and most popular alcoholic beverage, it literally brings to the table thousands of years of historical significance and a few (possible) health benefits. And even naysayers who object to the use of alcohol in sport must agree with the empirical data that points to this well-substantiated premise: Beer rocks.

The basics of brew are simple. All types of beer share the same ingredients: water, malted barley, yeast, and hops. After that, the choices are practically endless. The number of brands, styles, and formats in the beer category is enough to make any player almost ready to put down the ball. Almost.

To help navigate the dazzling array of options, we've created a three-step process for picking the best beer not for plank-roasted salmon, but for the optimal game of Beer Pong.

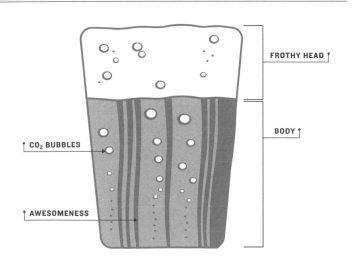

FROTHY HEAD ↑

BODY ↑

↑ CO_2 BUBBLES

↑ AWESOMENESS

TOP LAGERS TO PLAY WITH

· · · · · · · · · · · · · · ·

▷ Pilsner
▷ American-style
▷ Oktoberfest
▷ Bock (beware high alcohol
   content)

STEP I. Choose the beer best described as "ice cold."
Forget spicy hop infusions or subtle caramel notes in dark-roasted malts—all that really matters is temperature. Chilly perfection measures exactly 39 degrees Fahrenheit.

STEP 2. Look for a lager.
Beer comes in just two basic forms: ale and lager. Ale is an older style and often offers an earthier, more complex flavor profile. Great for pints, but not for sporting purposes. Lagers—lighter, smoother, and more effervescent—are the preferred style for Beer Pong.

STEP 3. Buy American first.
The best sporting beer is easy to drink, popular with all players, and widely available. American brewers come through on all three counts—and it is only fitting to honor the country that produced this sport. If you explore beyond the country's borders, we recommend that you select brands that can be pronounced without affecting a French accent.

Cans vs. Bottles vs. Kegs

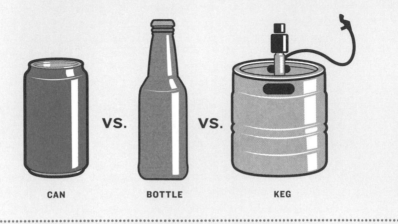

CAN   BOTTLE   KEG

CANS
PROS: Opaque metal blocks light, which causes skunkiness. Easy to transport and clean up. Comes in convenient 30-packs. You can stack them in a fridge to pack more in.
CONS: When a can is dented, the highly acidic brew can eat away at the aluminum and infuse your beer with a putrid *eau de can.*

BOTTLES
PROS: Everything tastes better out of a bottle. Bottle caps are cool to collect and make a great addition to your table. Glass is highly recyclable. Bottle can be used as an impromptu play-by-play microphone
CONS: Bottles are more expensive than cans, and 10 times heavier, adding to transportation costs. Bottles can break and cause serious injury.

KEGS
PROS: The beer flows and flows like the Ganges River. Draft beer is considered by experts to have the best taste. You can have a keg toss contest once it's empty.
CONS: Kegs are expensive and heavy. You need a tap. Requires *a lot* of ice.

THE TABLE

This is probably the most important piece of equipment in the sport. The ideal and classic standard is a traditional table-tennis or Ping-Pong table measuring 9 feet long, 5 feet wide, and 2½ feet high. If a standard-size table-tennis table is not available, try to use a surface or table with similar dimensions. Or make your own.

THE KEG-AND-DOOR TABLE

WHAT YOU'LL NEED:
- Two kegs
- One door

This is by far the easiest and quickest way to get a table. Simply remove a door from its hinges and place it across a few supporting kegs. If kegs or a door are not easily available, you can substitute an oversized windowpane on sawhorses, a mattress on six bar stools, or a metal road plate on two orange traffic barrels (not advised).

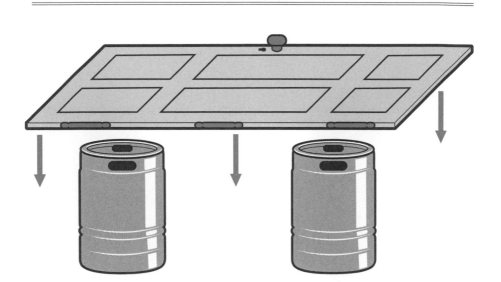

THE CUSTOM TABLE

Want to make something a bit more substantial? Try this easy method, using materials that can be found at any local hardware store.

WHAT YOU'LL NEED:
- Six 24-inch two-by-fours (end rails)
- Four 30-inch two-by-fours (end rails)
- Four 84-inch two-by-fours (side rails)
- One piece of plywood, 48-by-84 inches and $1/2$ inch thick
- One box of 3-inch screws
- One box of 2-inch finish nails
- Drill
- Wood putty
- Paint
- Polyurethane
- Bottle caps and adhesive (optional)

STEP I. Assemble the end rails.
Each end rail consists of two 30-inch two-by-fours and three 24-inch two-by-fours. Assemble the pieces as shown on the next page and attach using screws. Pre-drill the holes for the screws so that the screw head is recessed into the two-by-fours. You will need to make two end rails in total.

STEP 2. Assemble the side rails.
Take the remaining 84-inch two-by-fours and attach them to the end rails using the screws as shown on the next page. Be sure to pre-drill again to make sure the heads are recessed. The finished product should resemble a rectangular wooden frame.

STEP 3. Place the plywood top onto the finished base.

Rest the 48-by-84-inch plywood onto the base making sure it is centered all around. Nail in place using the finish nails.

STEP 4. Painting.

Once the table is complete, use the wood putty to fill in all the exposed holes on the base and top surface. Coat the entire table with your favorite paint color. Have fun with colors and design.

STEP 5. Polyurethane.

Once the paint dries, spread a light coat of polyurethane across the top surface to protect the table from the inevitable spills that will occur during game play.

OPTIONAL. Bottle caps.

To take this table to the next level, you can apply bottle caps to the top surface. The best way to attach the caps is to coat the top surface with a thin layer of epoxy or use Liquid Nails to attach each cap individually. Arrange the bottle caps in any pattern you like. Once the caps are in place and the adhesive dries, cover the caps with polyurethane to protect them from rust.

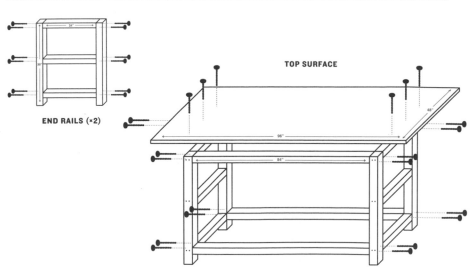

END RAILS (×2)

TOP SURFACE

SIDE RAILS (×2)

THE PROFESSIONAL TABLE

If you don't have the time or space to build your own table, you're in luck. Hundreds of entrepreneurs have begun to create and sell professional Beer Pong tables. Most Pro Tables are lightweight, easy to set up, and simple to fold up for easy transportation—or hiding. When looking for one to purchase, make sure to keep these criteria in mind.

1. Length and height.
You don't want a short and/or low table.

2. Construction and durability.
You don't want a table that will blow away in the wind or buckle under the weight of the racks.

3. Price.
Remember, you get what you pay for.

Optional
EQUIPMENT

As you can see, Beer Pong requires relatively little equipment to get started. However, when you are ready to take your game to the next level, you can add some of these accessories to enhance your Beer Pong pleasure.

THE RACK

Developed by GetBombed.com, the Rack is a convenient cup holder that helps you establish a perfect rack every time and keeps cups from spilling and knocking over. Even better, you can place the cups in the rack, carry it directly to the beverage filling station and bring the game-ready rack back to the table to start playing. This is a must-have piece of equipment for any serious player.

SHOOTING LINE

Basketball has a free throw line, darts has the oche (pronounced "ockey"), and even bowling has a lane line—so why not have an official line for Beer Pong? A shooting line will eliminate disputes over elbows, leaning, and edging shooters. As with most things in life, all you need is duct tape. Place a piece on the ground behind the table a standard step back from the edge on both sides.

LIST AND BRACKET

Everyone wants to play next. The only way to keep track is to have a list that players fill out—first come, first served. As teams lose, cross off their name and the next team in line plays. This keeps games running smoothly and eliminates disputes. When having a tournament, make sure to create a bracket that clearly outlines who plays whom and how the progression works.

PITCHER

At an event that's blessed with the presence of a keg, nothing helps speed things along better than a good pitcher. The on-deck team should fill it up prior to the start of their match so games can continue seamlessly. Nothing is worse than having to wait forever to get your cups filled. Be prepared.

ZAMBONI

During the course of a match, the table tends to get wet and slippery. To avoid a rack catastrophe, keep a roll of paper towels, a rag, or towel nearby to wipe up any spills.

BREATHALYZER

As explained previously, Beer Pong is not a drinking game. Intoxication and the sweet taste of victory do not mix well. That said, the strategic, controlled application of alcohol can help loosen one's game and calm one's nerves. It is not uncommon for serious players to employ a breathalyzer to help monitor this delicate balancing act.

REFEREE

To settle disputes at the table, nothing works better than having a referee to oversee the match. Designate a person—the designated driver is a good choice—to oversee all matches. This newly crowned official needs to be an expert on the game. If they've read this book, they're a good candidate.

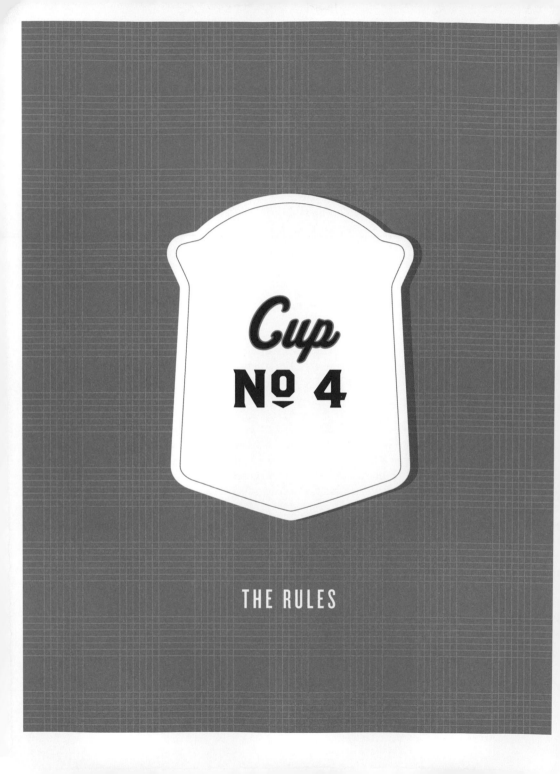

Cup
Nº 4

THE RULES

ONE OF THE REASONS FOR BEER PONG'S STUNNING RISE IN POPULARITY IS ITS FREEFORM, DECENTRALIZED NATURE.

HOUSE RULES HAVE PROLIFERATED as different groups established their own regulations. From state to state, even from block to block, the rules of engagement change, bend, and morph. However, due to Beer Pong's rising fame and overwhelming demand to legitimize the sport, it is critical to establish a set of universal standards. And in doing so, we're about to delve into the most controversial aspect of Beer Pong: rules.

We have scoured the country, surveyed players, polled leagues, and consulted with experts in order to compile the most comprehensive set of rules ever formulated—a code of conduct that provides a basic foundation for game play. We humbly propose that they be adopted by everyone. Not only will this decrease the number of heated debates and soured friendships, but it will also make it easier for players from across the country to square off—creating a more playable and less intimidating sport.

Of course, we still support the creativity inherent in regional, local, and personal variations. And in the next chapter, Cup #5, we will introduce you to some of these innovations, along with fun additions and sometimes-ridiculous side rules you might use to create your own house rules. But first, let's lay down the law.

1. THE PLAYERS

1.1. Each team consists of one (1) or two (2) players, but both teams must have an equal number of players.

    1.1.1. A two-player team is the most common and preferred format.

    1.1.2. Players on a team must remain consistent throughout the game.

    1.1.3. Substitutions are allowed in medical emergencies only and must be approved by the other team. If not approved, the game is forfeited.

2. THE EQUIPMENT

2.1. The Table

    2.1.1. The table should be a flat, smooth surface with no dividers or other objects on the surface.

    2.1.2. The ideal table is a table-tennis table measuring 9 feet long, 5 feet wide, and 2½ feet high.

    2.1.3. If a standard-sized table is not available, the surface must be as close as possible to those dimensions.

2.2. The Balls

    2.2.1. The game is played with two (2) 40-millimeter table-tennis balls.

    2.2.2. The host is expected to have at least four (4) balls on the premises to compensate for lost or damaged balls.

2.3. The Cups

    2.3.1. Standard 16-ounce disposable plastic cups are to be used.

    2.3.2. If non-standard cups are used, all rack cups on both sides of the table must be identical.

3. THE SETUP

3.1. The Cup Allocation

    3.1.1. Twenty-two (22) cups are to be procured for each game.

    3.1.2. Twenty (20) cups are employed for the racks, 10 per side.

    3.1.3. Two cups are employed for wash cups, 1 per side.

3.2. The Rack: Each team shall defend 10 live cups arranged in formation.

    3.2.1. The standard starting rack is a pyramidal shape—the back row has four cups, the next row has three, the next has two, and the top has one.

    3.2.2. The cups must be level and tight (touching).

    3.2.3. The back row of cups should rest about 1 inch from the back edge of the table.

    3.2.4. The rack must be placed as close to center as possible (with equal space to the left and right of the cups).

    3.2.5. None of the cups shall be tilted, lopsided, or leaning on surrounding cups.

3.3. Beverage Distribution

    3.3.1. The fill line of the cups should be determined prior to the start of the game, and each side should have an equal amount of the beverage in every cup.

    3.3.2. The recommended allowance is two fluid ounces per cup (approximately two 12-ounce cans per rack).

    3.3.3. As a default measurement, one of the ribs on the side of the cup may be designated as the universal fill line for that game.

3.4. Wash Cups

    3.4.1. Each team shall have one (1) dedicated wash cup filled with approximately 12 ounces of warm water to clean off the ball.

    3.4.2. Before each throw, the ball should be cleaned in the wash cup.

    3.4.3. The wash cup can be refreshed at any time during a match when it becomes too dirty to perform its duties.

    3.4.4. The defending team can request the replacement of the wash cup one (1) time during the game.

3.5. The Shooting Plane

    3.5.1. Before the first shot, it is critical to define the shooting plane—the area from which legal shots are attempted.

    3.5.2. One step back from the end of the table is regulation when using a standard-size Beer Pong table.

    3.5.3. If a shorter table is being used, the players should determine the legal shooting plane by measuring the distance and marking the ground.

THE SHOOTING PLANE SHOOTOUT:
STEPS VS. ELBOWS

••••••••••••••

There is clearly a need to standardize participants' shooting position to avoid unfair advantages and claims of impropriety.

One common method is the Elbow Rule, which states that a player's elbow may not cross the edge of the table. The benefits are obvious: Elbows are plentiful and easy to locate. The downside, however, is the risk of game-ruining debates. The violation occurs for only a split second, and judgments are affected by viewer angle.

By establishing shooting position based on foot location instead, the playing field remains level—and the game can go on.

3.6   Challenges to Setup

3.6.1. Disputes over the quality of equipment and consistency of beverage-in-cup distribution between the teams should be brought forth prior to the start of the game.

3.6.2. If a team does not feel the game can be played in a fair, equitable manner, they are permitted to leave the premises prior to the start of the game.

3.6.3. If entrance fees were paid to the organizer, full refunds—as well as insults from the rest of the teams—are in order.

HOW MANY CUPS DO YOU PLAY WITH?

••••••••••••••

1. **10 cups**. 80%
2. **6 cups** 17%
3. **Other** 3%

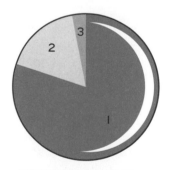

*GETBOMBED.COM SURVEY RESULTS

4. GETTING STARTED

4.1. Prior to the start of play, there are three (3) options to determine first possession.

    4.1.1. Random chance: The two teams may use a method of random chance (coin toss, rock-paper-scissors, odds or evens) to determine how the game starts. The winner will have two options: to start the game or to pick their side of the table. The opposing team takes the remaining choice, and teams can proceed to set up at opposite ends of the table.

    4.1.2. Snake eyes: One player from each team starts with a ball. They stare each other in the eyes and simultaneously shoot the ball at the rack. If both players miss, the other team members do the same, alternating until a cup is sunk. If both players sink a cup, then it cancels out and snake eyes continues. If one player makes a cup and the other player misses, the team of the player who hit the shot gets both balls to start. The cup that has been made remains in play and is not removed.

    4.1.3. Winners first: If previous games have been played, the winning team in the previous game shoots first.

5. SHOOTING

5.1. Each team will take turns shooting two (2) balls a side per turn.

    5.1.1. If playing doubles, each player shoots one ball each.

    5.1.2. If playing singles, each player shoots twice.

    5.1.3. A shot can be made in any fashion as long as it is not intentionally aided by an outside factor.

    5.1.4. Once the ball leaves the shooter's hand, the shot is in play, even if the shooter loses control of the ball.

5.2. A shot can come in one of two forms.

    5.2.1. Air shot.

        5.2.1.1. An air shot is when the ball is thrown directly at the cups, without an intervening bounce on the table.

        5.2.1.2. An air shot cannot be defended until it hits the surface of the table or a cup.

5.2.2. Bounce Shot.

    5.2.2.1. A bounce shot is when the ball is thrown intentionally to hit the table before bouncing toward the cups.

    5.2.2.2. Once the ball hits the table, it can be blocked by the defending team in any way, including smacking, catching, swatting, and air punching.

HOW DO YOU SCORE BOUNCE SHOTS?*

•••••••••••••••

1. **Bounces count as 2 cups (you can block)** 87%
2. **Bounces count as 1 cup (no blocking)** 7%
3. **Bounces count as 1 cup (you can block)** 6%

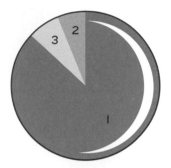

*GETBOMBED.COM SURVEY RESULTS

---

6. SCORING

6.1. Sinkage

    6.1.1. A ball is considered "sunk" if it enters any of the opposing team's cups and contacts the surface of the beverage contained within that cup.

    6.1.2. If a shot knocks over a cup, that cup is counted unless it is obvious that the ball has not entered the cup (it may have hit the side of the cup).

    6.1.3. If the shot bounces off the defending team member's person or clothing and gets sunk, the shot shall be counted as sunk.

    6.1.4. If a shot is attempted during cup removal and interference occurs, the shot is replayed.

    6.1.5. If a shot enters the cup, spins around clockwise or counter-clockwise and then leaves the cup, it is not considered sunk.

6.2. Removal

6.2.1. Once a ball is "sunk" in a cup, the defending team must immediately remove the "sunk" cup.

6.2.2. The contents of the cup shall either be drank from the rack cup or transferred into a separate "chill cup" for consumption.

6.2.3. Players on two-person teams should alternate the removal of cups.

6.2.4. Empty cups shall be placed off the table and are out of game play.

6.2.5. When a shot has been sunk by an air shot, one (1) cup is to be removed.

6.2.6. When a shot has been sunk by a bounce shot, two (2) cups are to be removed.

6.2.6.1. The first cup removed shall be the one sunk cup; the defending team has sole discretion over which cup shall be removed as the second.

6.3. Bring-backs

6.3.1. If a team sinks both of its balls in one turn, that team gets both balls back and shoots again. This is called a bring-back.

6.3.2. If one or none of the bring-back balls are sunk, then the other team will take their turn to shoot.

6.3.3. If both bring-back balls are sunk, the shooting team will get both balls back and shoot again.

DO YOU PLAY BRING-BACKS?*

●●●●●●●●●●●●●●●●

1. Yes—both players get to shoot again (unlimited) . 61%
2. No 16%
3. Yes, but only one shot 12%
4. Yes—one shot, and if it goes in, you get another shot (alternating until someone misses) 12%

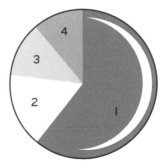

*GETBOMBED.COM SURVEY RESULTS

7. RE-RACKS

7.1. Cups may be consolidated or "re-racked" into smaller triangles at two points during a game: when there are six remaining cups (racked, from back row to front: three cups, two cups, one cup) and three cups remaining (2,1).

    7.1.1. Players shall not shoot until the opposing team clearly finishes re-racking.

    7.1.2. Always center the last cup and position it about 1 inch from the back edge of the table.

7.2. The team on offense must request the re-rack from the opposing team.

    7.2.1. If a team fails to request a re-rack at the appropriate time and proceeds to sink another cup, they miss their re-rack opportunity and must leave the cups as are until the next point of re-rack.

HOW MANY RE-RACKS DO YOU PLAY?*

1. **One re-rack** 28%
2. **Two re-racks** 52%
3. **Three re-racks** 7%
4. **More than three re-racks** . . . 9%
5. **None** 4%

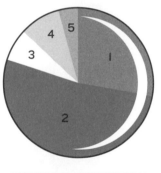

*GETBOMBED.COM SURVEY RESULTS

8. DEFENSE

8.1. A player may swat or catch a ball ONLY after it has made contact with the table surface or a cup.

    8.1.1. You may not interfere with a ball anytime before it makes contact with any surface.

    8.1.2. A one-cup penalty shall be enforced for premature swats and grabs.

8.2. If during the course of defending, the ball is deflected by the defender's body into a cup, or the defender bobbles, swats, or hits the ball into one of his own cups, that cup is considered sunk and must be removed by the defending team.

8.3. If during the course of defending, a defender knocks any cups over, those cups are counted as being sunk and must be removed from the table.

8.4. If a defender makes physical contact with the rack during an attempt at defense and the shot ball does not become sunk in a cup, the defending team must remove one cup from their own rack. The shooting team shall pick the cup to be removed.

9. DISTRACTIONS

9.1. A distraction or attempted "psych-out" is permitted at any time during a match.

9.2 A defender may attempt to distract a shooter by any means necessary as long as no contact is made with the cups, rack, ball, table, or the opposing team.

    9.2.1. Causing the flooring to shake or generating an air current to alter the ball's flight path, while indirect, is forbidden.

9.3. If during a distraction the shot bounces off the defending team member's person or clothing and lands in a cup, the shot shall be counted as sunk and that cup shall be removed.

10. INTERFERENCE

10.1. Cup Interference

    10.1.1. A player may touch the cups only to remove a sunk cup, to re-rack, to reposition drifter or orphan cups, or to prevent a cup from falling over. Any other touch is considered interference and shall result in a one-cup penalty.

    10.1.2. If a player accidentally or intentionally knocks over any number of his own team's cups, those knocked-over cups are considered sunk and must be removed.

10.2. Ball Interference

    10.2.1. Any contact, accidental or intentional, with the ball before it hits the table or cup is considered interference and shall result in a one-cup penalty.

10.3. Outside Interference

    10.3.1. If interference is caused by a non-player, an animal, or an act of God, the shot shall be replayed.

BEER PONG FACTOID

A drifter or orphan cup is a cup that mysteriously moves out of position on its own due to slippery conditions.

11. END OF GAME

11.1 Rebuttals

    11.1.1. Once a team has sunk its last cup, the opposing team is allowed an additional turn to sink their competitors' remaining cups. This is called the rebuttal round. The last cup is not to be removed until rebuttals have failed.

11.1.2. If, when one team has sunk its final cup, the opposing team has more than one cup remaining, the Gentleman's Rule goes into effect:

    11.1.2.1. Each player gets to shoot until he misses. This means a single player can sink all the remaining cups so long as he doesn't miss.

    11.1.2.2. Once the first player misses, his partner gets the same opportunity.

    11.1.2.3. If the second player also misses, the game is ruled over.

11.1.3. If, when one team has sunk its final cup, the opposing team has only one cup remaining, play proceeds as follows:

    11.1.3.1. If the final cup was sunk in one turn, the rebutting team gets only one shot.

    11.1.3.2. If the final cup was sunk on a second turn, the rebutting team gets two shots.

11.1.4. If at the end of the rebuttal round the rebutting team has not made all remaining cups, they lose and the game is over.

11.1.5. If the rebutting team sinks all their remaining cups, the game goes into overtime.

HOW DO YOU SHOOT REBUTTALS?*

••••••••••••••••

1. **Each player shoots till they miss**
   (Gentleman's Rule). 60%
2. **Each player gets one shot each** 24%
3. **Alternate one shot per player**
   (unlimited bring-backs) 15%

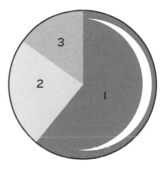

11.2. The Spoils

    11.2.1. The losing team must consume its remaining cups as well as its opponents' remaining cups.

    11.2.2. It is up to the losing team to decide the distribution of beverages between the team members.

12. OVERTIME

12.1. When a game goes into overtime, a new three-cup pyramid is set up on each side of the table, and the first team to sink its final cup during regulation time starts with the balls.

    12.1.1. Original rules apply.

    12.2.2. The number of overtimes is unlimited.

13. DISPUTES

13.1. If there is no rule in place for a given situation, then a redo shot shall take place.

13.2. If a player thinks a rule has not been followed, that player can appeal to an outside spectator agreed upon by both teams.

    13.2.1. The outside spectator shall not be biased in his decisions, and if in doubt of his or her own objectivity, can appoint a replacement to settle the dispute.

    13.2.2. If the outside spectator cannot resolve the issue, then a redo shot will be allowed.

    13.2.3. A player can appeal at any time and as much as he/she wants.

    13.2.4. If a player or team asks for too many appeals which are not valid, the outside spectator has the right to place a restriction on both teams or refuse any more appeals to that individual team or player.

13.3. If a player refuses to abide by a ruling, he or she may be ejected from the game.

    13.3.1. If the ejected player is part of a two-person team, the remaining player may ask the other team to find a replacement; if no replacement is available, the remaining player must forfeit.

    13.3.2. If both players are ejected, the team automatically forfeits.

13.3.3. A player cannot be ejected without first being given a warning.

13.3.4. A warning can be issued only to a specific member of a team, not to the team as a whole.

13.4. If a player or team decides not to abide by the rules that have been established and the two teams cannot resolve the issues, then the the game is to be abandoned.

13.5. If a player becomes a danger to himself, other players, or spectators, he is to be ejected by all of the other players, including his own teammate.

NOTES

Beer Pong Etiquette 101

10 RULES FOR BEING A POLITE AND PROPER PLAYER

1. **KEEP YOUR RACKS ON THE LEVEL.** Make sure your racks are tight and touching, with no loose, lopsided, or tipping cups.

2. **FILL YOUR CUPS PROPERLY.** Two ounces of beer per cup is standard. Don't underfill any cups, as this will lead to knock-overs.

3. **ALWAYS CLEAN YOUR BALLS.** Clean your ball off in the wash cup or wipe it down before you shoot. No one wants to find dirt in their cup.

4. **TAKE A STEP BACK.** When you shoot, don't crowd or edge the table. Take a step back from the edge before you shoot. If you lean while shooting, stand back even further.

5. **NEVER SHOOT DURING A RE-RACK.** Wait until the other team clearly finishes re-racking before you shoot.

6. **DON'T STACK EMPTY CUPS.** Instead, use the waterfall method. Line them up side by side as they're removed. This will reduce funk transmission and keep them clean.

7. **CHANGE THE WATER CUP.** Do this as often as possible—we recommend before every match. Consider a vodka and spring-water solution for maximum germ fighting.

8. **WIPE OFF THE TABLE.** Keep the table surface dry at all times. No one wants to play on a slippery and dirty cesspool.

9. **BE READY FOR THE NEXT MATCH.** If you are next on the table, make sure to get enough beverages and cups ready to go for both teams before the previous match ends.

10. **DON'T POCKET THE BALL AND CUPS.** When the match is over, don't leave the table with a cup or the balls. This will not only delay the next game but might get you blacklisted as an equipment burglar.

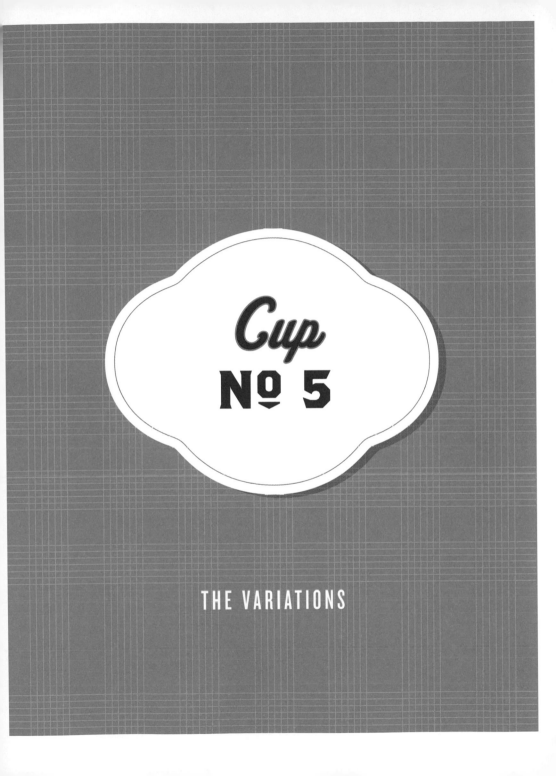

Cup
№ 5

THE VARIATIONS

THE SPORT'S LAWS ARE WRITTEN. IT IS TIME TO BEND THE RULES. OR USE A CROWBAR AND GO MEDIEVAL ON THEM.

IN KEEPING WITH THE SPORT'S underground roots and decentralized growth, it's no surprise that many players personalize their Beer Pong experience. To some, the basic rules of the sport are an open-source platform: available for others to build from, to develop, and to generally confuse the situation.

Many a "ringer" has fallen victim to venue-specific regulatory variations. If you get involved in a potentially contentious match without having clarified all the details, you have only yourself to blame. So to help you be prepared to face even the most unusual of house rules, we have attempted the daunting task of cataloging and explaining as many of the seemingly infinite variations on Beer Pong rules as we could track down.

To do this, we've not only drawn upon our own collective years of Beer Pong experience, but we've also utilized a multitude of media to survey the Beer Pong-playing public, yielding a plethora of rule variations that you can choose to use, laugh at, or modify to suit your own "house rules." Remember, while our coverage will be ample, it would be impossible to discover every individual rule fluctuation, let alone list them in this book. So no crying if we neglect to mention your [insert funny rule here].

Remember, while specifics may change from game to game, the single most important rule never changes: Obey the house rules. Whoever is running the night's festivities has the God-given right to do whatever the hell they want. To paraphrase General Douglas MacArthur, "Rules are made to be broken—rewritten and taped to the wall before the night's games."

Rack VARIATIONS

So much depends upon a plastic cup. It is the sport's literal and figurative goal. And, like everything else in Beer Pong, the players have the liberty to rearrange, reconfigure, and ultimately reinterpret the rack to fit their own playing styles.

CUP SETUPS

At first glance, it might not seem like there's much room for creativity. And it's true that more than 80 percent of players use the standard 10-cup pyramid setup. But that means 20 percent are out there exploring the great unknown. Here are a few other orientations you can use to start.

THE 6-RACK

Beginners and those strapped for time might choose to start with this smaller pyramid. It lends itself to quicker games that get closed out after a shooting streak.

TWELVE-CUP DOUBLE RACKS

Sometimes teams will choose to set up two separate six-cup racks in front of each player. The separate racks get combined into one rack when six cups remain. Typical re-racks for this version occur at six and three cups.

THE GREAT PYRAMIDS

Twenty cups on each side are stacked on top of each other in the form of two large three-dimensional pyramids. Savvy players will attempt to parlay this into extra credit for their Egyptian history class.

THE CENTURY

This is the mother of all racks—100 cups per side. The preparation time and initial cup investment are significant. Many consider it to be like a monster truck: visually impressive, but ultimately impractical.

RE-RACKS

Some players find it acceptable to re-rack on formations other than the standard six- and three-cup re-racks. If you do choose to deviate from the norm, just make sure it is known prior to the start of the match what re-racks are acceptable and how many are allowed. That being said, here is a rundown of the various re-rack scenarios that could occur in a match.

6-RACK, AKA WARM-UP

5-RACK, AKA AZTEC

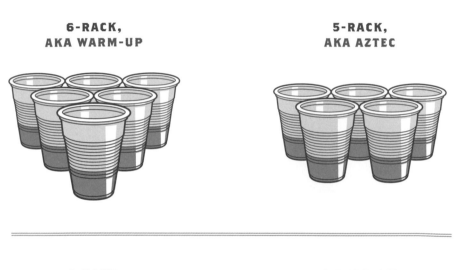

4-RACK, AKA DIAMOND, SHA-DIAMOND

4-RACK ALT, AKA SUPER DICK

3-RACK,
AKA TRE

3-RACK ALT,
AKA BIG DICK

2-RACK,
AKA DICK, DICK 'EM,
DOGGY STYLE

1-CUP,
AKA KARL

VARIABLE RE-RACKING OCCASIONS

COURTESY RACK

If a team requests a re-rack even though they have used up their given number of racks, the defending team has the option to grant an additional re-rack. This altruistic gesture typically occurs during lopsided beat-downs and rebuttals.

MID-RACK

A mid-rack is a re-rack that occurs after the first player on a two-person team shoots. In other words, it happens midterm—after the first player's turn, and before the second's.

NO MID-RACK

Basically, this rule states that you cannot re-rack mid-turn. For example, if there are seven cups remaining and the first shooter hits a cup, leaving six, the second shooter cannot request a re-rack before their shot. However, if player No. 1 misses and player No. 2 makes it, they will get the re-rack at the beginning of their next turn. If both players make it, they get balls back but miss the re-rack.

COACH SAYS

When re-racking the last cup, always move it to the back edge of the table and center it between both corners.

Game Play
VARIATIONS

Documenting every house rule in the Beer Pong world is beyond the scope of this book—and the attention span of its authors. But a handful of common variations recur with enough regularity to warrant a closer look.

THROWING PATTERNS

Sometimes, players decide to play with a throwing pattern different than the traditional two shots per team. Some examples:

ONE-BALL

Shots alternate one shot at a time per player per team. So, for a game between Team A (players 1 and 2) and Team B (players 3 and 4), the throwing order might be: A1, B3, A2, B4, and so on.

SPEED PONG

This variation is used with a set number of balls (usually two), and there is no throwing pattern. If a cup is missed, whoever can grab the ball first gets to shoot it. This style of play is often mentioned in the same sentence as "mêlée," "free-for-all," or "eye gouge."

BRING-BACKS

If you want to put a different spin on the traditional two-ball bring-back, try one of these variations:

BABY-BACK

Only one ball is returned on the bring-back.

CALLED SHOT

If you call a shot at any time and make it, you get to shoot again. However, if you call a cup and make it into a different one or miss, you get a one-cup penalty.

ONE-AND-ONE

Similar to a baby-back, but if the shooter makes their third shot, they get the ball back and continue alternating shots with their teammate until someone misses.

HOW TO HANDLE AN AIR BALL

··················

If a shot completely misses all the cups and goes over the end or either side of the table without any contact whatsoever, the shot is considered an Air Ball.

When a player shoots an air ball, they must remove and drink one of their own cups. (Although, you cannot lose the game this way.)

This variation just barely made our official rules section, but it rimmed out of contention due to its overly Draconian punishment of novices. But experts are encouraged to employ it at large parties to keep the games moving— and the egos deflated.

BONUS CUPS

In some variants of the game, certain shots in addition to bounces may count for more than one cup.

DRIFTER OR ORPHAN CUP

This cup is named for its tendency to slide once in a while on slippery or uneven surfaces. If you sink a ball in one of these cups while it's moving, the other team must remove that cup along with one other.

SKILL CUP

A skill cup is a cup isolated from all the other cups. For example, if the two cups in the second row have been removed, the front cup would be isolated. If the player who is shooting calls "Skill cup" and sinks that cup, the defending team must remove that cup and one other. If the player misses or makes a different cup, no cups are removed. In some Beer Pong circles, a bounce shot into a skill cup counts as a triple-cup sink. You cannot end the game on a skill cup, and you're allowed only one skill shot per cup.

WATER CUP

If a player calls the defending team's water cup and makes the shot, the defending team must remove two cups. If the player misses, there is a one-cup penalty.

TOUCHING CUPS

If both players on a two-person team sink a ball in the same cup, all touching cups are also removed. For example, if both shooters hit the front cup on a full rack, then that cup is removed along with the two touching cups behind it. Although cups are to be removed as soon as they are sunk, sometimes players forget or are too slow to remove a cup. So, quick shooting is necessary to perform this controversial rule variation.

INSTANT WINS

There are some Beer Pong permutations in which a "game over" rule is incorporated. In these variants, a player can instantly end a game with no rebuttals if certain situations arise.

DOUBLE CUPS

If there are only two cups left on the defending side and both shooters on a two-player team sink shots in those cups during the same turn, the game is over with no rebuttals.

DOUBLE TAP

If there is only one cup remaining and both players on a two-person team sink the last cup during the same turn, the game is over with no rebuttals. When this rule variation is in effect, the last cup must remain on the table until both shots are attempted.

RING OF FIRE, AKA CIRCLE OF DEATH

If a team hits the front cup (head cup), the two back corner cups (dunce cups), and the center cup (bitch cup) before any other cups are sunk, that team automatically wins.

SAME CUP

At any time during a match, if you and your teammate make both of your shots in the same cup before the opponents move that cup, you automatically win.

SNIPER CUP, AKA DEATH CUP

If a player is holding a cup that has not been drunk and the opposing team hits that cup, the game is over. Player is allowed to move their cup, or swat the ball, making it critical to try to sneak the shot in when they're not paying attention.

Besides the basic defense techniques such as distraction, grabbing, and swatting, some players utilize more direct means of defending a shot. There are two common methods to remove a ball that is still spinning inside the cup. These are controversial and should be played only with honest players.

BLOWING

A ball spinning inside the rim of a cup but that has not become sunk can be considered still in play, and may be defended by blowing it out of the cup using your mouth.

FINGERING

Similar to blowing, except the player uses a finger to flick the ball out of the cup. The proper method involves a slightly bent finger form and a scooping motion that does not catch nor trap the ball. It is important to note that there should be only one active finger making contact with the ball.

RESTRICTED DEFENSE

These rules place limits on when defense can be played, if at all.

DRINK FIRST

This rule states you can't play any defense until you drink a sunk cup. Basically, if a cup is sunk and you're holding that cup while your opponent shoots, you can't block the next shot. If you do, it counts as a sunk cup and you have to remove the cup. If it's a bounce attempt, you must remove two cups.

LET IT RIDE

This format is much like the NBA All-Star game, since no defense can be played, period—no swatting, grabbing, blowing, or fingering.

HOW TO BLOW A GAME—DEFENSIVELY

. . . .

1. Make sure you qualify according to the house rules. Blowing is a tactic often extended only to female players. If you are not sure, ask your host about the rules—and your general practitioner about your gender.
2. Establish position early. Since it is only legal to blow while the ball is in motion, it helps to have your head close to the rack in anticipation.
3. Approach at an angle. A directly vertical air column may only push the ball down. So try to direct your breath at an angle of approximately 42 degrees.
4. Beware of splash-back. Collateral damage of beer foam on the face is a common downside of this tactic.

DO YOU ALLOW BLOWING OR FINGERING?*

. . . .

1. Yes, but only guys can finger and only girls can blow 58%
2. No—it's not allowed 26%
3. Yes—anything goes 16%

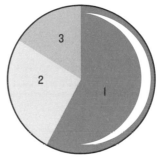

*GETBOMBED.COM SURVEY RESULTS

Tournament-Specific Rules

There's a big difference between house games among friends and seriously organized tournaments with an entry fee. According to Billy Gaines, founder of the World Series of Beer Pong (WSOBP), you might want to consider implementing a few rule modifications when hosting a large tournament.

These rules are designed with three purposes in mind:
1. Fairness to all players
2. Efficiency in running a maximum number of games simultaneously
3. Minimizing disputes between participants

Having run the largest tournament in the world, and having spent hundreds of hours debating potential playing variations, Billy suggests the following rules:

BRING-BACKS

In general, if both players on a team sink shots on the same turn, that team will get one (1) additional bring-back shot, not two. Either teammate may take the bring-back shot.

> GAINES: *"The first WSOBP was played without bring-backs, but we (and the players) missed them. After some heated debate on the Bpong.com forums, Dustin Pope—the fool that became our close friend when he almost could not compete in WSOBP I because he lost his wallet between checking into the hotel and walking to his room—suggested that we have one-ball bring-backs. Thus, we had the solution, and we named it the Pope's Rule, because we could."*

BOUNCING

Players are allowed to bounce their shots, but if they sink the ball it counts as only one cup. You are not allowed to defend or block a bounce.

> GAINES: *"One of the memorable moments of my Pong career was playing some pong at the soccer players' house. Some old clowns showed up, commonly known as alumni. Despite us giving them a hard time, these clowns bounced. Their reasoning: That's how they played the game 'back in the*

day,' so they weren't going to let us young'uns tell them how to play the game. Thus, it occurred to me, and sticks with me to this day: Who the hell are we at the World Series of Beer Pong to tell people how to shoot the ball?"

LEANING

Leaning is permitted, with the following exceptions:

(a) Players may not place a hand/foot/leg/genital on the table in order to gain additional reach and/or leverage. Of course, if you have a beer gut that must rest on the table because there's nothing else you can do with it; the "beer gut on the table" exception will apply.

(b) Players may not edge themselves around the table to throw.

(c) Players may not remove their feet from the ground while throwing, unless it is a regular part of their throwing style and they are not excessively leaning.

GAINES: *"It comes down to fairness. With big money on the line, we have to be fair, and we've got to get it right. Determining whether a person's elbow crossed some imaginary line is semi-subjective. What if it's the championship game and maybe that guy's/girl's elbow crossed the table? I make the wrong call, I cost a team $50,000 (or more). I don't want that."*

DISTRACTIONS

Distractions are allowed. However, the players may not cross the plane of play (back of the table) with any part of their bodies. No player may intentionally disturb the air surrounding the cups in play, such as by fanning with hands, hat, or any other objects. No visual blocking of the cups is allowed. Blinding of the opponent's cup, such as with lights or a laser pointer, is not allowed and will result in ejection.

GAINES: *"Just let the team shoot, damn it. Do I really need to explain this?"*

When a sport places control of governance in the hands of the greater player community, it is no surprise that some of those changes defy categorization. It is also no surprise that some of those rules involve running around buck-naked.

BEHIND THE BACK

If a shooter can grab his own rebound from a missed shot while the ball is still on the table, he is allowed to shoot again, but the shot must be attempted from behind the back.

BITCH CUP

If a team sinks the center cup (bitch cup) first, it doesn't count. In other words, the first cup sunk cannot be the bitch cup.

HOT HANDS

If the first shooter on a team sinks a cup, he has the option to take the team's second shot as well and to continue to shoot until he misses. Obviously, his teammate must agree to this, and forfeits his own turn if his teammate misses. You can relinquish Hot Hands at any point and turn the shot back over to your teammate.

"ON FIRE," AKA NBA JAM RULE

Invented by the video-game generation for the video-game generation, this rule mimics a feature in the eponymous game. It states that upon a player's making two consecutive shots, he must proclaim that he is "heating up." If he then sinks a third consecutive shot, he can proclaim that he is "on fire." At this point, the game is paused as the player receives unlimited shots until he misses. Once he misses, the game continues.

SHUT OUT, AKA SKUNKED, BLUNTED

If the losing team has not sunk any cups, they must perform a dare given by the owner of the house. Examples include running around the house naked, drinking from your shoe, or making out with your partner.

Game Play
VARIATIONS

These are similar to television show spin-offs. Some are successful, like *Frazier* from *Cheers*. Some are more like *Joanie Loves Chachi*. But regardless of their popularity, they all offer more ways to encourage mastery of the skills of the sport.

THREE-MAN KNOCKOUT

A team is made up of three players, and in front of each is a triangle of three cups. Once possession is determined, each team gets one shot per player per turn. The object is to knock off all three players by eliminating the three cups in front of each. Once all three of a player's cups are gone, that player is eliminated. Play continues until all players on one side are knocked out. The team with any amount of players left wins.

FULL-CONTACT PONG

Not for the weak or timid, this game is a no-holds-barred free-for-all. If a shot is missed, any player may attempt to get the loose ball by any means necessary—diving, tackling, clotheslining, etc. Whoever gets the loose ball gets to shoot. Be warned: Excessive damage, spilled cups, broken tables, and serious injury can occur. So play this version at your own risk, but do so wisely, carefully, and by all means, capture it on video.

STRIP PONG

As the name implies, this is the Beer Pong version of strip poker. While it does insert nudity into the already utopian mix of Beer Pong ingredients, it also adds a scar—an exposed scar—to the game. It reinforces the negative party stereotypes, it places disproportionate priority on socializing rather than sportsmanship, and it generally detracts from the credibility the sport has established.

That said, you might still want to play if the opportunity should present itself. Here are a few possible variations:

1. Each cup has an article of clothing written on the bottom of it. After the cup is made for the first time, the defender can choose to drink said cup or to remove said item. If the cup is made a second time, the clothing *must* be removed. The cup is also removed.
2. More simply, every hit cup can result in the removal of the cup and an item of clothing.
3. Finally, the most basic way to play is to simply get naked and play a game—until someone calls the cops.

BEER BASEBALL

This is just like a game of baseball: nine innings, three outs per inning, and in the end, the team with the most points wins.

First, get two teams with an equal number of players. Then, on each side of the table, set up four cups in a straight line along the table's lengthwise centerline; place an additional cup off to the side on the edge of the table. Fill each cup with beer—start by filling the cup farthest from the opposing team with the most fluid, then fill each subsequent cup with less than the one before it. The cup off to the side may be filled to the level of your choice.

Sinking a ball in the first cup counts as a single; the second, a double; the third, a triple; and the last, a home run. A missed shot is counted as a strike. Three strikes is considered an out. Players get on base by sinking a particular cup. The cup off to the side is a steal cup. At any time when there is a runner on base, a member of the runner's team can grab the steal cup and chug it. As they do, the other team has to grab their steal cup and chug it as well. The first person to finish their drink and then flip cup the cup onto the table earns the steal or gets the out. During the seventh inning, "Take Me Out to the Ballgame" must be sung at neighbor-waking levels.

H-O-R-S-E PONG

Based on the popular basketball variation, this one-on-one game is driven by pure one-upmanship. Players set up at opposite ends of the table and arrange five cups in a single row along the back edge of each side of the table. Alternating single shots, players aim at their opponent's cups. If a player sinks a cup on his turn, his opponent must sink the same cup in his setup. If he misses or sinks a different cup, that cup is removed. If he sinks the same cup, that cup remains in play. Continue taking turns until winner has no cups left to sink.

LOB PONG

Lob Pong uses paddles and is derivative of traditional table tennis, mirroring many of its rules and techniques when it comes to serves, faults, and scorekeeping. Game play is exactly like traditional table tennis, with the only difference being that half-full beer cups are placed in each corner of the table. Players can score either by the traditional rules of table tennis or by hitting or sinking one of the cups. If a player hits an opponent's cup, that's not only a point for the player, but the opponent must also sip the beer. If a player sinks a ball into a cup, it counts as two points for the player and the opponent must drink the beer and replace it with a fresh one. The game is over when a player reaches 21 points.

SLAM (FAST) PONG

A faster, more aggressive version of Lob Pong, this variation combines aspects of both table tennis and volleyball. Each team consists of two players: a server and a slammer. The server sets up the ball for the slammer, who sends it rocketing toward the other team's cups. Unlike Lob Pong, scoring is based primarily on landing the ball in or near the cups, with a different variety of points and cup consumption methods being awarded based on whether the ball hits a cup, sinks into a cup, or knocks one over.

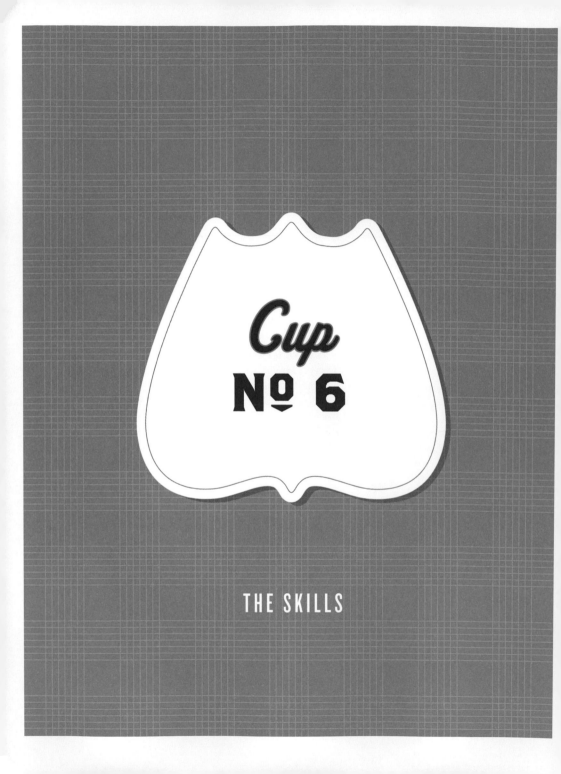

Cup
№ 6

THE SKILLS

NOW, IT IS TIME TO TAKE THAT STEP FROM AVERAGE TO ALL-STAR— IN BEER PONG AND LIFE IN GENERAL.

YOU'VE LEARNED ABOUT BEER PONG'S HISTORY and what it's become today. You've studied its rules and equipment. Now you are ready to put this knowledge into action. More specifically, into the action of sinking some balls and handing out beat-downs.

As in any sport, the path to greatness is through complete mastery of a set of fundamental skills. Since the basics of the sport have developed organically and often underground, it should be no surprise that there have never been any formal guidelines for training. No summer camps, no private lessons, no 12-CD infomercial systems.

Until now, that is.

We've analyzed, dissected, and documented the techniques that countless Beer Pong crusaders have dedicated their lives to protect—how to hold, how to throw, how to stand. And in this chapter we also offer valuable insight into the concentration techniques and other mental skills that the game requires.

Most Beer Pong masters would not dare share this information with you until you had been training for years and were deemed worthy of such insider knowledge. But we're about to reveal the "Shaolin secrets" of the sport.

History's greatest competitors, from Muhammad Ali to Michael Jordan to Andre the Giant, have all agreed that success comes from a combination of physical precision, mental acumen, sound preparation, and intestinal fortitude. It is our hope that the advice to follow will help maximize the potential for greatness of a whole new generation of Beer Pong athletes— including players like you.

THE PHYSICAL *Skills*

The premise appears so simple: Put the ball in the cup. But the reality is that this simple act requires a player to execute a series of movements with precision and fluidity to ensure that shots are made consistently—on the mark and in the foam.

To expedite the tutelage in physical form, we've broken down the action of playing into the following basic units:

1. **THE GRIP**: *Holding the ball in the proper manner*

2. **THE STANCE**: *Maintaining proper footwork and form*

3. **THE FLIGHT PATH**: *Comparing the different possible trajectories*

4. **THE AIM**: *Determining the optimal destination selection*

5. **THE SHOT**: *Putting it all together*

6. **THE DRINK**: *Consuming the contents of your cup*

NOW, LET'S EXPLORE EACH OF THESE GAME-BUILDING UNITS IN GREATER DETAIL.

THE GRIP

The ball grip is one of the game's most critical elements. It's what controls accuracy, speed, and ball spin. When analyzing form, this is where the rubber meets the road—or more accurately, where the fingertips meet the plastic.

While fad sports like "golf" and "tennis" focus great attention on just a few different grips, Beer Pong enthusiasts employ a far greater variety, which allows for a larger range of motion and a wider arsenal of choices for any game-time challenge.

TRADITIONAL GRIP, AKA DA GRIP, BASIC OVERHAND, BOB

The ball is held between the thumb and forefinger, resting on the middle finger for stability. The release comes with a quick snap of the wrist to produce slight backspin. This grip works with all stances and shooting styles. Popular and effective, it is a must for anyone trying to play the game. In short, this is the missionary position of ball grips.

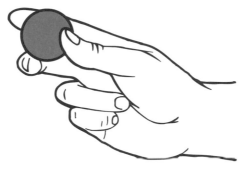

TRIGGER GRIP, AKA OVERHAND HOOK, BUSTA KAPPA KAPPA

In this variation on the traditional grip, the ball is held between the tip of the thumb and the entire index finger, but the middle finger is now turned down—resting for post-game use. Since this shot does not generate much spin, it can cause shots to run wild—especially during outdoor play where wind can be a factor.

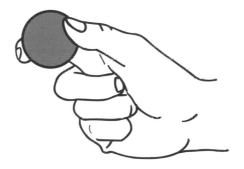

ROYAL GRIP, AKA MACK DADDY, DADDY MACK

This difficult grip involves a pan-digit approach, with the ball held between the thumb and all four fingers. The ball is thrown backhanded, and proper throwing motion can produce an impressive amount of backspin—and spectator wows. The term royal refers to either the crown of fingers surrounding the ball or the grip's popularity among sovereign autocrats.

UNDERHAND GRIP, AKA BOCCE GRIP, UNDERDOG

As in the Royal Grip, the ball is held between the thumb and all four fingers. The main difference is that the hand is inverted to throw the ball underhanded. When properly executed, the toss will create tremendous backspin, making this a solid grip for outdoor matches.

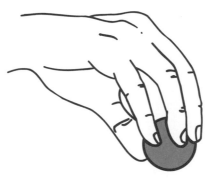

F-U GRIP, AKA GAME OVER, IN YOUR FACE

This one is pure intimidation. The ball is held between the thumb and middle finger and held up high for all to see. This grip is usually broken out as a finisher to end a game with authority. But be warned, if you attempt this grip and miss, you might as well step off the table and hang up your drinking shoes for good.

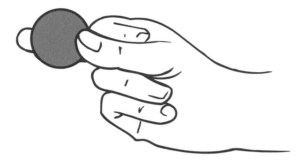

ALL-PRO QUOTE

I use my middle finger and my thumb. I feel more comfortable, and I have more control over the ball with those two fingers. I think some of that comes from playing baseball in college. I controlled most of my pitches using my middle finger on different places on the ball and was very accurate in doing so.

—NEIL GUERRIERO,
2007 World Series of Beer Pong Champion

CLAW GRIP, AKA STINKY PINKY, TEA TIME

The thumb and first three fingers are used in this professional-grade grip. When properly released, it can generate significant spin and curve. It may be hard to control at first but is very effective once mastered, and is highly recommended for windy outdoor play. During High Tea Pong, the pinky may be extended.

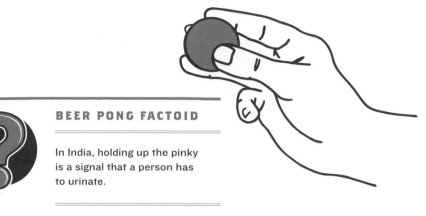

BEER PONG FACTOID

In India, holding up the pinky is a signal that a person has to urinate.

PEACE-OUT GRIP, AKA ROCK-PAPER-SCISSORS GRIP, HIPPIE GRIP

An even rarer variation on the Royal Grip, this grip uses just the index and middle fingers. When shooting the ball, release it quickly and smoothly with a slight—but still manly—snap of the wrist. It can be used with a backhand or overhand throw.

GRANNY GRIP, AKA LOB, SEMI-PRO

The ball is gently cradled in your hand like a delicate flower. The ball is tossed in a smooth underhanded swing. When mastered, the toss will create no spin whatsoever, which makes this a good opening shot for a full rack. Fortunately for players who use this grip, there are no style points in Beer Pong.

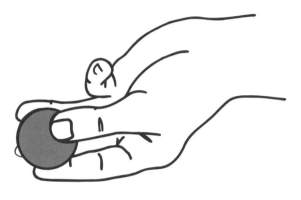

THE STANCE

The next step in improving and perfecting your shooting percentage is your stance. This is the foundation upon which to build your championship-caliber shot. When choosing and developing your stance, just remember that accuracy begins with firm footing—by figuring out your own personal equilibrium, you will feel more comfortable and get the most benefit from a good stance.

Just keep in mind the rule that says your elbow must never go past the edge of the table at any time during your shot. This is referred to as the Elbow Rule—perhaps one of the most controversial and hotly debated aspects of the sport.

There is no conclusive evidence that breaking the table's invisible plane during your shot actually accomplishes anything. But refraining from doing so ensures that your opponents will not have an excuse to protest and avoids the inevitable game-ruining debate. With that in mind, the smart play is to step back (an arm's length) from the edge of the table before you set up your stance. Your respect for etiquette will not go unnoticed.

To get your game off on the right foot, the following is an overview of the four most common stances.

REGULAR STANCE

First, identify the foot that corresponds to the hand you intend to shoot with. Now, place this foot forward and perpendicular to the table. Place your other foot at a 45-degree angle behind the forward foot, in a position that allows you to distribute your weight evenly. If you do not feel balanced, spread your feet farther apart. Stand up straight, with your shoulders back but comfortable and in line with the center of the cup you are aiming at.

Leaning too far forward can lead to back injuries over time, so be aware of any strain or pain after throwing. To paraphrase Mr. Miyagi, "Balance is key. Balance good, everything good. Balance bad, better pack up, go home."

GOOFY FOOT

Stand with your feet shoulder-width apart with the foot opposite from your shooting hand in the forward position—thus the term "goofy," a phrase typically associated with surfing and wakeboarding, two other sports in which it's best to avoid face-plants and swallowing too many liquids. Point your front foot toward the cup you are aiming at. Your foot should be extended forward slightly with your knee bent. Take your other foot and place it behind you with just the ball of your foot touching the ground. Most of your weight should be on your front foot to get optimal balance. Stand with a slight tilt forward and in line with the cup you are aiming for. Avoid excessive use of boarding jargon such as "amped," "stoked," or "gnarly."

COACH SAYS

If you don't bend your knees slightly, you will have a hard time getting the ball to go straight every time. Bend them too much and you'll have difficulty replicating that position.

FREE THROW

Position both feet behind the table. Make sure you are standing directly in front of the rack. Place both feet straight toward the cups, feet shoulder-width apart, being careful not to angle either foot to the left or the right, lest you brick your shot harder than Ben Wallace. Stay in position and do not walk away from the table until the shot is at the cup. Exchange assorted low-fives and ass slaps with teammates and/or spectators when the ball is sunk.

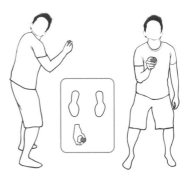

COACH SAYS

When you throw, move only your throwing arm. Any extra movement in your stance will make it nearly impossible to shoot consistently. And impossible is not in your vocabulary, remember.

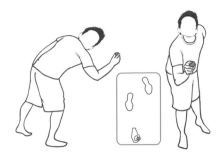

THE LEAN

This is a controversial stance that overtly challenges and disregards the Elbow Rule. So if you're going to use it, be sure to either set up far enough back from the table or make sure there is no Elbow Rule in play. Set up as you would for the regular stance and then lean your body as far forward as you can without losing your balance. It's hard to keep your balance, so make sure you are stable.

COACH SAYS

Balance is the most important element to any good stance. If you can't keep your balance, change your stance.

THE FLIGHT PATH

Controlling your shot's arc can make the difference between landing your ball in the foamy bed of your opponent's beer or unceremoniously rimming it out in defeat. From the moment the ball leaves your hand, gravity is in control. However, you can predict the ball's flight path by taking into account the direction, points of contact, and strength of your release before handing it over to the universe and Sir Isaac Newton.

Obviously, the velocity of your throw determines how long or short the shot is. But it's important to consider how much impact the angle of entry has on your sinkage rate (the percentage of shots made) and cup margin (the mathematical size of the rim that the ball faces as it enters the cup). When you take into account how much these factors affect whether you make a shot, this section might well be the most critical to your game.

ANGLE OF ENTRY

It has been said that Beer Pong is a game of angles. (Ironic, since it has caused many a math class to be missed.) Before proceeding, it is important to introduce the concept of angle of entry.

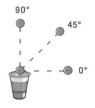

90° SHOT

In a straight-down, 90-degree shot, the actual and apparent rim sizes would be equal. Shooting from this angle will yield a 100 percent cup margin and 100 percent sinkage rate. In other words, a correctly placed shot would go in all the time. Unfortunately, it's impossible to achieve, since you can't drop your ball from directly above the cup, no matter how far you lean or how freakishly long your arms are.

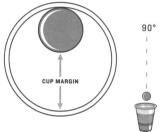

APPARENT RIM VIEW

CUP MARGIN

0° SHOT

Conversely, if you have a 0-degree arc, you will have a 0 percent cup margin and 0 percent sinkage rate. You would front-rim it every time, and it would be impossible to make a cup. You'd be the Chicago Cubs of Beer Pong.

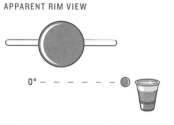

APPARENT RIM VIEW

OPTIMAL° SHOT

The optimal arc of your shot should fall within a 30-to-70-degree range. Obviously, your cup margin and sinkage rate will vary with the angle of entry. Keep in mind that physics proves it is more difficult to control distance when shooting with a higher arc. However, the higher the arc, the better your chances are at making a cup. So if you can control your distance, this is the best flight path, mathematically speaking.

APPARENT RIM VIEW

CUP MARGIN

THE OTHER FACTORS

Now that we have a grasp on cup margin, it's important to understand the other main influences that affect a shot's flight path:

CONTROL—*the thrower's ability to aim and place a shot*

TOUCH—*how much oomph (or mustard) is on the shot, which determines how it reacts to hitting the cup*

VARIABILITY—*how susceptible a shot is to fluctuation given game conditions. Unlike control, which is based on the thrower's ability, variability is determined by factors that will be referred to as "other things"—providing convenient excuses for why you missed a shot.*

COACH SAYS

There are only four ways to miss: long, short, left, right. Five, if you include plain sucking.

ALL-PRO QUOTE

I have a very high arcing shot with a slight twist in my fingers when I release. I also try to do the same thing every time, including approach, shot, and follow-through.

—NICHOLAS VELISSARIS,
2006 World Series of Beer Pong Champion

THE PATHS

Here is a rundown of the basic flight paths categorized, analyzed, and alphabetized.

THE ARC

The most common flight path involves the ball moving along a gentle parabola.

ANGLE OF ENTRY: High
Allows the thrower the highest angles and thus the largest cup margin on the market.

CONTROL: Irregular
Here's the rub: The higher the arc, the harder it is to control the distance of the shot.

TOUCH: Soft
In general, it provides a lighter touch that reduces rim-outs and increases rim-ins.

VARIABILITY: Moderate
The arc shot is the most susceptible to influence from air currents and air resistance. Use caution if playing outside or near powerful HVAC equipment.

WHEN TO USE: This technique is your best chance, mathematically, to sink a cup. Take care to balance the height of your arc with your ability to control it. Our studies have shown that an arc shot arriving at approximately 68 degrees is optimal—allowing for both control and cup margin while providing ample time for the crowd and your opponents to admire your shot before it lands in the cup with the plop of victory.

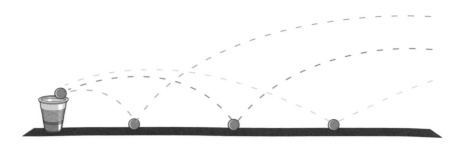

THE BOUNCE

A bounce is performed by—surprise—bouncing the ball toward the cups.

ANGLE OF ENTRY: Low
The low trajectory is achieved by bouncing the ball in a sideways motion.

CONTROL: High
This one's similar to the line drive, only you are aiming for a spot on the table.

TOUCH: Soft
It's like butter when the ball gently limps over the lip of a cup.

VARIABILITY: High
First, the quality of the bounce is dependent on the quality of the table surface. Second, some rules allow a bounce to be swatted away.

WHEN TO USE: Unless you are the Chris Paul of Beer Pong, this can be a difficult way to put the ball in its home. That's why some rules make it worth two cups. If you are kicking butt and taking names, the bounce can be a great finishing move to add insult to injury. If you are down, it can be a quick way to catch up in the cup count. In short, if bounces count as two cups, try it; if they only count as one, why bother.

THE LINE DRIVE

This dart-style shot follows a quick and direct line to the intended cup.

ANGLE OF ENTRY: Low
The angles are lower, therefore so is the cup margin—and the margin for error.

CONTROL: High
Experienced players find that this forceful shot is the easiest to maintain control over.

TOUCH: Hard
Due to the velocity of this path, friendly bounces are few and far between, and rim-outs are to be expected.

VARIABILITY: Low
With its high velocity through the air, this shot is the most consistent.

WHEN TO USE: The line drive is like an overpowered sports car: If you can keep it on the road, you'll be successful—and get more dates. But if your shot is not 100 percent on the mark, don't expect the kind hand of physics to help you. Tall players can have more success with this one, since their height increases the entry angle. Break out this technique when wind is a factor (high winds = low arc).

THE AIM

Proper aim is imperative to sinking cups. It sounds simple enough, but like many aspects of this sport, once you drill down, you unearth unexpected levels of complexity and nuance. In this case, we'll uncover two primary aiming techniques.

THE RACK AIM

Many beginners focus on all of the cups in the rack when shooting. Simply lob the ball across the table in the general direction of the middle of the rack. For real players, this is the equivalent of shooting with your eyes closed.

PROS:
- WORKS WELL WITH A FULL RACK
- OFFERS ROULETTE-STYLE SURPRISES
- WELL-SUITED FOR PEOPLE WHO DON'T CARE ABOUT OUTCOME

CONS:
- FALTERS ONCE THERE ARE GAPS AND SPACES IN THE RACK
- DOESN'T LEAD TO WINNING
- SUCKS

COACH SAYS

Don't be called a "rack shooter" or a "chucker"—aim for a cup!

THE CUP AIM

A good player will *always* focus on a specific cup. This is clearly the most basic way to develop and maintain throwing accuracy. This is what separates a clutch player from your average Joe.

PROS:

▷ WILL PAY OFF LATE IN GAME WHEN THERE ARE ONLY A FEW CUPS, AND WHEN THE CUPS ARE SEPARATED

▷ MINIMIZES MISSED SHOTS AND IMPROVES CHANCES OF SINKING AN UNINTENDED CUP

▷ MAKES SINKING THE LAST CUP NO DIFFERENT THAN ANY OTHER CUP

CONS:

▷ TAKES SOME PRACTICE AND FOCUS

ALL-PRO QUOTES

I always have a cup strategy. Depending on the rack, I always aim for a specific cup on that rack.

—NEIL GUERRIERO,
2007 World Series of Beer Pong Champion

Usually me and whoever I play with shoot turns based on the formation of cups. You have to give your partner the chance to get a bring-back or hit a big shot to build your partner's confidence if they're not playing to their ability.

—MICHAEL POPIELARSKI,
2009 World Series of Beer Pong Champion and
7-time World Beer Pong Tour Champion

Eye and Hand Dominance

In Beer Pong—as in second-tier sports like archery, darts, and golf—good hand-eye coordination is critical to one's success. The relationship between sight and shot is much more sophisticated than it may appear on the surface. The first step in harnessing this spiritual connection in your own body is figuring out your eye-hand dominance correlation.

DETERMINING YOUR DOMINANT EYE

1. Extend both hands in front of your body.
2. Place hands together, making a diamond between your thumbs and your index fingers.
3. With both eyes open, center an object across the room in the diamond (for example, a stack of copies of this book).
4. Close your left eye. If the object remains in view, you are right-eye dominant. If the reverse is true, you are left-eye dominant.

DETERMINING YOUR DOMINANT HAND

1. Place a pong ball on top of a stack of copies of this book.
2. Reach out and pick up the ball.
3. If you picked up the ball naturally with your right hand, you are right-hand dominant. If you used the left hand, you are left-hand dominant.

RESULTS:

ALIGNED DOMINANCE

Eye and hand dominance are aligned on the same side of the body. This is known in the Beer Pong industry as "normal." When aiming a shot, your sightline and throwing position can be perfectly lined up.

CROSS-ALIGNED DOMINANCE

In this condition, your dominant eye and dominant hand are on opposite sides of the body. In the parlance of the game, you are "weird." This could cause fluctuations in your performance accuracy and frequent shanking of shots.

But there is help. Simply being aware of your condition will improve your game as you make small adjustments to compensate. You can also try training your lazy eye with an eye patch worn over the dominant eye during practice. This will build a more natural eye-body coordination and will likely improve the consistency and accuracy of your game. As an added bonus, you may be able to use your newfound pirate persona to distract your opponent at game time.

THE SHOT

Our dissection of the mechanics of a shot, while thorough and groundbreaking, may cause some readers to think that the perfect Beer Pong throw is merely a series of movements performed in succession. In fact, the completed shot is much more than the sum of its parts. It's a graceful orchestration of muscles, joints, and cartilage—working together under the watchful conductor of your brain.

To help you master the Byzantine complexity of the Beer Pong shot, we've created a simple acronym to encapsulate the totality of this world-class technique. We call it our BEEER method.

B = Balance
E = Eyes
E = Elbow
E = Extend
R = Remember

BALANCE. MAKE SURE YOU ARE BALANCED BEFORE YOU ATTEMPT A SHOT.

Your first thought should be about settling yourself and positioning yourself as consistently as possible. Find something on the floor with which to line up your front foot, and use that as a guide. Then check your weight distribution—stay off the toes, since they're harder to keep steady. Remember: Inebriation can wreak havoc with your equilibrium, so employ the consumption strategy known as "moderation."

EYES. DIRECT YOUR EYES TO A SPECIFIC CUP WHILE YOU SHOOT.

A focused aim on one specific cup is better than shooting at the whole rack. Train your focus on the back rim of the cup so that you are basically looking through the cup. Ignore the desperate gyrations of your opponents, and the hottie off to the side of the table.

ELBOW. KEEP YOUR ELBOW IN TOWARD YOUR BODY WHEN SHOOTING.

After you have your balance and focus set, line up your elbow so that your shooting arm forms an "L" shape beneath the ball. This keeps your movements along only one plane, reducing shot variability and general not-winning-ness.

EXTEND. STRAIGHTEN YOUR ARM AS YOU RELEASE THE BALL AND FOLLOW THROUGH.

If your follow-through is consistent, it will improve your overall form. After you release the ball, keep your hand up in the air as if you were reaching into a bag of spicy barbecue potato chips held out in front of you. Your hand and arm should look like the head and neck of a goose in flight.

REMEMBER THE FIRST FOUR POINTS.

Shooting the Angles

Many sunk cups are either unintended or collateral damage from a missed attempt, an over- or under-shot, or a rim-out. To maximize these "collateral cups," adjust your shooting angle by shifting your stance so that you are directly lined up with the greatest number of cups, including the one you are aiming for.

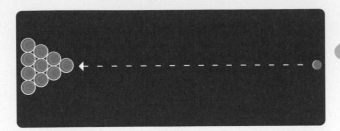

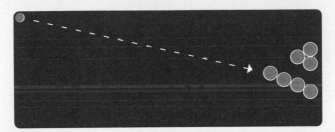

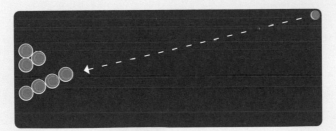

THE DRINK

The drinking component of Beer Pong is often taken for granted—due to the fact that swallowing is an ingrained human reflex. But a few tips will help the cups go down easier.

I. POUR INTO A DESIGNATED DRINKING CUP.

As discussed earlier in this book, players should consider the use of a dedicated drinking cup—also known as the chill cup—to reduce saliva and other funk transmission. An additional benefit is that it allows some of the carbonation in the beverage to dissipate. Not only will slightly flatter beer be easier to drink, it may also decrease post-game "stomach music."

2. DEFOAM THE BEER.

A "head" on a beer is caused by the rapidly expanding carbonated bubbles rising to the top. Introducing an oil to the mix reduces the surface tension of the bubbles, causing them to collapse. Fortunately, the pores on your nose provide your own strategic oil reserve—simply swipe your clean index finger between your nose and cheek then swirl it in the foamy head.

3. COMPRESS THE SIDES.

One of the benefits of using the standard all-American plastic cup is the ability to optimize your drinking form. Grip the midsection of the cup and squeeze gently. This creates a sort of spout that directs the fluid into your mouth cavity and not on your cheeks, neck, shoulders, and chest.

4. RAISE THE SIGNAL.

Place non-drinking hand above head and extend index finger skyward. It is rumored that this opens your rib cage, allowing for improved flow-through. But this is probably wrong. What is factual, however, is that it lets everyone know that you are taking care of business.

5. DRINK.

6. PROCLAIM YOUR COMPLETION.

An important part of drinking mechanics is a sudden exhalation of air from the lungs. As the air is coming out, many players decide to form a phrase that signifies their completion.

PRACTICING YOUR SKILLS

Winning separates the professionals from the amateurs. And what makes them win is that they're better. And what makes them better? Genes. But if you don't have the genotypic gift of Beer Pong greatness, you can always practice your way to the top—or as high as your talent will take you. Here's a six-point plan for developing your greatness.

I. PICK A TECHNIQUE AND MASTER IT.

There's no point shooting hundreds of different shots if you are doing it the wrong way. Practice a variety of grips, stances, and throwing techniques until you find a combination you are comfortable with. Then use that form, and only that form, for every game.

2. DEVELOP A ROUTINE.

Like every basketball player at the free throw line who is not named Shaq, you should have a ritual that helps you focus your energy. Something as simple as touching the edge of the table twice or rolling the ball in your hand can help create an isolated period of concentration before you let it fly.

3. PRACTICE SHOOTING AT DIFFERENT CUPS.

If you keep shooting at the middle cup, you'll be a perfect rack shooter, but you'll be sub-optimal at all other cups. Practice by spacing out three cups randomly on the table. Once you have sunk all three, rearrange the cups in a different formation.

4. CREATE A DRIVING RANGE.

This is the complete opposite of the game experience: no distractions, no waiting, no time to overthink. Just get a bucket of balls and simply focus on mastering your form, shot after shot. Keep your stance planted to remove that variable. Notice how your mechanics evolve as fatigue and/or boredom take over.

5. CROSS-TRAIN.

Developing your game sometimes requires that you broaden your skill set in order to bring new elements—and ultimately advantages—to your game. Consider taking up darts, table shuffleboard, or bowling. All involve mastery of form, and an occasion to drink and play simultaneously. Plus, they keep you inside and away from the damaging UV rays of the sun.

6. PLAY A LOT OF BEER PONG.

You can never get enough practice. Gather up a few friends in the basement or walk down to the local watering hole, and play some games. Try to practice a couple of times a week. Pay attention and listen to your partner. Keep a journal of your games and how you felt after each performance. Hide this journal to avoid being made fun of.

ALL-PRO QUOTE

We practice by playing. We always aim at single cups and in certain patterns, every game, no exceptions, so we really don't feel we need to practice outside of just playing the game the way it should be played.

—JEREMY HUGHES,
2008 World Series of Beer Pong Champion

WARMING UP

Any great athletic effort requires preparation. Marathon runners do deep knee bends. Pianists limber up their fingers. Kobayashi eats heads of lettuce. Beer Pong athletes, too, must make warming up a part of their routine before every game, as well as during the off-season (that is, weekdays).

THE BENEFITS OF WARMING UP ARE OBVIOUS. BUT IN CASE YOU DIDN'T KNOW:

> ▷ IT LOOSENS UP MUSCLES AND GETS THE BLOOD FLOWING TO YOUR THROWING HAND.

> ▷ IT DE-STRESSES THE BODY AND FOCUSES YOUR MIND ON THE TASK AT HAND: BEER PONG.

> ▷ IT CAN HELP PREVENT REPETITIVE STRESS INJURIES LIKE "PONG ELBOW" BY PREPARING THE JOINTS BEFORE THE ACTION.

Below are four simple exercises to help increase your physical control and decrease injury.

I. SPIDER PHALANGE

Put your hand flat on a wall in front of you. Use your fingers to "climb" up the wall (like a spider). Every few inches, stop and hold your hand in place for 30 seconds. Keep going until your fingers are as high up the wall as you can reach.

2. THE BUDDHA PONG

Place both palms together in a praying position at chest level. Keeping your palms in contact with each other, bring both wrists downward. Continue to separate palms, and feel the stretch in your fingers. Try to bring your palms parallel to the floor when keeping your fingertips together.

3. TWELVE-OUNCE SHOULDER SHRUG

Hold a 12-ouncer in each hand, arms by your side. With arms down, shrug your shoulders in a circular motion—forward, then back. Do not rotate your arms above shoulder level, as that will only add additional stress to your joints—and shake up the beers.

4. THE ROCKY IV

Move to rustic cabin in a secluded area of Russia. Run through snow. Chop wood. Lift an ox cart. Beat the big Russian. Rinse and repeat.

WAYS TO PLAY IT SAFE

·················

- ▷ Drink plenty of water before and after the game.
- ▷ If you feel pain, apply two 12-ounce ice packs to the affected area.
- ▷ If you see 20 cups across the table, stop playing.
- ▷ Never drive or get in the car with someone who has been drinking.

Beer Pong's physical demands are obvious to both players and spectators—clearly that ball isn't going to sink itself. But equally crucial to one's success at Beer Pong is mastering the game's mental component.

The mind certainly is a terrible thing to waste—especially since it plays such a large role in success at the table. And occasionally in life, too. The final section of this chapter will focus on getting the most out of the three-pound organ above your neck.

RELAXATION

Beer Pong is not a game of brute force. It's a game of touch and finesse. (Note: We mean this in the most manly sense.) To achieve your best possible results, it's critical to be in a relaxed state. Unfortunately, some athletes go about this the wrong way, telling themselves, "This is only a game." Repeating patently false statements can only increase tension by wreaking havoc on your inner consciousness.

Instead, look to align your mind and body with a practice known as mindful breathing. It enables you to bring a sense of poise and calm to the most chaotic and high-pressure game environment. Here's how it works:

1. RIGHT BEFORE YOU THROW, FOCUS ON A BREATH THAT STARTS FROM YOUR BELLY.
2. INHALE THROUGH YOUR NOSE, FILLING YOUR LUNGS FOR A COUNT OF FOUR.
3. HOLD THE BREATH FOR A COUNT OF TWO.
4. EXHALE THE BREATH (AND TENSION) FOR ANOTHER COUNT OF 4.

Even one cycle helps you to focus on the present, to be more at ease, and to be less distracted by opponents making farting noises.

CONCENTRATION

This one may sound obvious at first—after all, what Beer Pong player worth their salt is not staring down the rack with fiery intensity and thinking through every possible bounce, skip, and roll? The problem is that much of this mental energy is misplaced. Here are a few ways to shift your paradigm:

I. DON'T OVERTHINK.

Thought is the enemy of accuracy. You need to concentrate but not overanalyze and obsess over what-ifs. In game situations, you need to be focused simply in the moment. Not on what may happen or what just did.

2. EMBRACE YOUR ROUTINE.

As discussed before, you must establish your pre-shot routine—the rituals that you perform every single time you throw a ball. Rely on this to ground you and give you something to focus on—other than the pressure.

COACH SAYS

Try to be on autopilot. Be sure to avoid paralysis by overanalysis. And avoid pinkeye while you're at it.

3. DON'T STARE AT THE RACK.

We're not advocating blindfolded Beer Pong—unless you are really good at it. But our research has shown that lengthy gazing at the target begins to cloud your visual perspective and increase stress levels. Instead, take a quick glimpse at the rack, then focus your eyes on the ball in your hand. Look back up at the cups only a split second before you throw.

4. DON'T TRY TO TUNE OUT THE DISTRACTIONS.

If you are actively trying to shut out your competitors' gyrations and "your mama" jokes, you are subconsciously feeding into these distractions. Instead, allow these gestures and taunts to figuratively go in one ear and out the other. Pay them little attention, and they will have little impact on your performance.

BEER PONG FACTOID

The human brain has about 100 billion neurons. The octopus brain has about 300 million neurons. We think we've made our point clear.

VISUALIZATION

Studies have proven again and again that visualization is a powerful tool for athletes. Groups that practice *and* use visualizations blow past those that only practice. This is due to the simple fact that the body reacts to imagined stimuli the same way that it reacts to real stimuli. Think hard enough about walking on a high tightrope and your heart rate will actually increase.

So before you shoot, close your eyes and try to see the ball making splashdown. Watch it happen in slow motion. Hear the swoosh of the perfect sinkage. Savor the victorious feeling you'll have as your opponents are lapping up their freshly sunk beers.

If your nerves are particularly frayed, try a surreal visualization. For example, imagine your arm growing eight feet long, reaching across the table, and dropping the ball softly into the cup. This should bring down your anxiety level by fooling the mind into thinking that the challenge at hand is an easy one.

POSITIVE THINKING

Getting mad at yourself for missing a shot really gets you nowhere. Negative thoughts compound, snowball, and ultimately become self-fulfilling prophecies. So it's imperative that you not work against yourself by applying the benefits of positive thinking to your game. Here's how:

1. DON'T FOCUS ON THE SHOTS MISSED.
Every ball is another chance to make a shot. You can't undo time, unless you have a time-traveling DeLorean. So put it behind you,

and embrace the ball in your hand as a winning shot just waiting to be released into the world.

2. DON'T ENGAGE IN NEGATIVE INTERNAL DIALOGUE.

We talk to ourselves every day. And sometimes the conversation is anything but upbeat. Try to listen for the defeatist phrases your mind is batting about and look to replace them with something nutritious for your peace of mind.

3. DON'T LOSE IT.

After a missed shot, avoid the urge to put your fist through the wall, crush the ball against your forehead, or sweep the table of all cups in a grand tirade. Such actions can have short-term therapeutic value, but usually result in physical injury, making an ass of yourself, and—worst of all—damage to the sacred Beer Pong playing gear.

COACH SAYS

Positive emotions have been shown to increase subjects' levels of inventiveness, perceptual focus, and skill acquisition. So having fun while you play may keep you from sucking so much.

Positive Psychological Cognitive Restructuring
FOR THE BEER PONG PLAYER

INSTEAD OF . . .	THINK . . .
"I'LL NEVER MAKE THIS SHOT."	"THIS SHOT IS MINE, AND I'M BRINGING THE NOISE AND THE FUNK."
"LAST CUP. ALL EYES ARE ON ME."	"LET'S JUST TAKE CARE OF THIS ONE LIKE ALL THE OTHERS."
"SHE'S REALLY DISTRACTING ME."	"I'M GOING TO MAKE THIS SHOT AND THEN GET HER NUMBER."
"I'M SO MAD I'M GOING TO BREAK THAT TABLE OVER MY KNEE."	"I THINK I'LL DO SOME ONE-ARM PUSH-UPS TO WORK OFF MY FRUSTRATION AND ENTERTAIN THE CROWD."
"I DON'T BELIEVE IN POSITIVE THINKING."	"THIS BOOK HAS CHANGED MY GAME AND LIFE. I'LL BUY TEN MORE."

Cup
Nº 7

THE FLAIR

IT'S TIME TO BRING THE FLAIR, THE STYLE, THE RAZZLE-DAZZLE, THE "SHAMA-LAMA-DING-DONG."

NOW THAT YOU ARE THOROUGHLY STEEPED in the essentials of Beer Pong, it's time to really spread your wings and stretch your legs. Or some combination of the two.

While other sports may look down on personal expression— even officially banning it in their killjoy rulebooks—Beer Pong encourages it. And that's not just in service of frivolous fun. As playwright Oscar Wilde once wrote, "In matters of grave importance, style, not sincerity, is the vital thing." But, we'd have to partially disagree with the playwright—and the editors of the quote book we pulled it from—and say this: Style *can* be sincere.

This is a key element to the sport. It's like the difference between still counting your steps on the dance floor and cutting the rug like a younger—and thinner—John Travolta. Likewise, truly playing Beer Pong requires more than merely going through the motions. Beer Pong requires that one exercise a little-known muscle called the heart.

In this chapter, we'll offer a survey of the various ways that you can bring style and flair to your game.

Distractions

The element of distraction is a critical part of the game. It brings the sport off the table and into the mind. It lifts it above mere skill and into the realm of strategy. This is part of the power and popularity of Beer Pong.

In other sports, taunting and antagonizing are considered poor sportsmanship and are left to the fans to implement and enjoy. But as a sport of the people, for the people, Beer Pong empowers players to do their own dirty work. Distractions are not just extracurricular—they're part of the very core of the sport. To begin your education, we present you with a range of techniques: verbal, nonverbal, lighthearted, and just plain wrong.

VERBAL DISTRACTIONS

Trash talk. Smack talk. Jiba jaba. Calling out one's opponent goes by many names. But they all get at the same idea: using words and phrases to get into your opponent's head and under their skin. With the advent of streetball, X-Box Live, and the whole yo-mama joke industry, today's Beer Pong athletes are probably well versed on the subject already. But we'll offer a brief over view just the same, to make sure you have the tools you need to properly talk a big game.

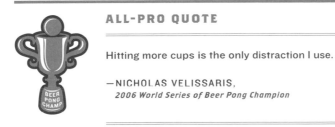

ALL-PRO QUOTE

Hitting more cups is the only distraction I use.

—NICHOLAS VELISSARIS,
2006 World Series of Beer Pong Champion

TRASH TALK
DOS AND DON'TS

•••••••••••••••••

DO assess the situation. Are your opponents friends or strangers? Are you playing for fun or for money? Are there weapons within reach? Calibrate your Smack-O-Meter accordingly.

DO decide on an approach. You can opt for constant, nonstop smack or a less frequent, more strategic approach.

DO turn it up. Regardless of your approach, always increase volume and voracity. Any reduction or backpedaling can smack of fear.

DO back it up. The best smack talk is served with a side of game. Michael Jordan reportedly ran his mouth the whole game. But he ran over the competition, too.

DON'T overstep. Know your opponents' limits to avoid making anyone go postal.

DON'T let the trash talk get too personal.

DON'T let it get physical. Let the head butt of France's Zinedine Zidane in the 2007 World Cup serve as a warning to everyone—and not just those with alliterative names.

DON'T stoop to racist or sexist remarks. It's hurtful and undermines the progress made in both the equal rights and Beer Pong movements. Plus, you might justifiably get your butt kicked.

ALL-PRO QUOTE

Although I choose not to use it much these days, trash talk is still an integral part of the game.

—JEREMY HUGHES,
2008 Word Series of Beer Pong Champion

TRASH TALK TO MAKE YOUR OPPONENTS MISS

▷ Running golf commentary. Talk to your partner as if you were providing the hushed color commentary of a golf broadcast.

▷ "Noonan!" Taken from the famous last putt scene of *Caddyshack*, you say "Noonan" right before your opponent throws. We don't, however, recommend quoting the whole damn movie all night.

▷ The "Miss it" cough. Pretend to be hacking up a lung but actually say "miss it" into your closed fist.

TRASH TALK AFTER YOU MAKE A SHOT

▷ "Nothing but foam!" Appropriated from basketball, this Beer Pong-specific phrase is self-explanatory in the context of the game.

▷ "Booyah!" This timeless expression stems from either a Belgium name for chicken soup or a shortened version of "booyakashah"—a Jamaican term for something.

▷ "That's what I'm talking about!" Not only is this well understood, it's apropos: You were in fact just talking about making that shot.

▷ "What's my name, fool?" Since "Who's your daddy?" officially jumped the shark, we'd like to recommend this phrase as a replacement. It was first heard from Muhammad Ali, who kept yelling it while winning a 1967 decision against Ernie Terrell.

OTHER POST-SHOT EXPRESSIONS

....

▷ "Count it like Chocula."
▷ "Did that just happen?"
▷ "Price is wrong, bitch."
▷ "That's right, son."
▷ "Call McDonald's, you just got served."
▷ "What?"
▷ "Drink it!"

NONVERBAL DISTRACTIONS

Studies show that more than 90 percent of communication is nonverbal. Our research into its role in Beer Pong has set this number at exactly 92.2344%. That's why it's crucial to make the most of your physical distraction techniques.

HAND DISTRACTIONS

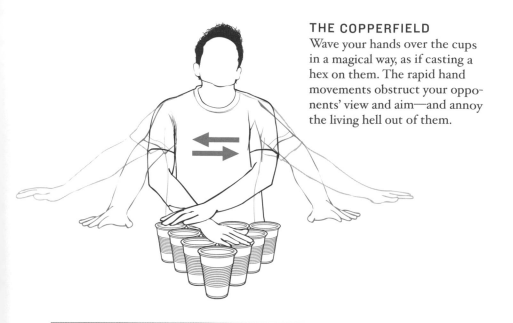

THE COPPERFIELD

Wave your hands over the cups in a magical way, as if casting a hex on them. The rapid hand movements obstruct your opponents' view and aim—and annoy the living hell out of them.

THE OCD RE-RACK

Claiming that the cups aren't properly stacked, the player poses as a Good Samaritan and pretends to constantly steady and position the cups to perfection.

THE AIR STEER

The distracter attempts to convince the ball to bend to one side through repeated two-hand wafting. While the physics of this are suspect, years of use in bowling and golf are proof of its effectiveness.

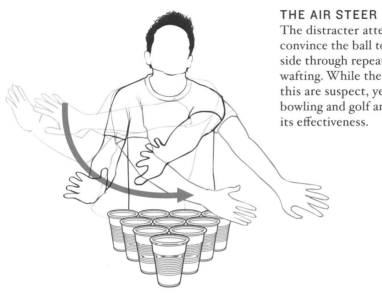

THE PHANTOM CATCH

Simply hold out your cupped hand several inches behind the table. It says, "You are going to miss it so I might as well catch it." It also stimulates the natural reflex for throwing a ball into an open hand that's innate in all humans.

FULL-BODY DISTRACTIONS

THE POP 'N' LOCK
The hypnotic effects of this move are amplified if you are really bad. For a demonstration, see the movies *Breakin'* or *Breakin' 2: Electric Boogaloo.*

PELVIC THRUST
Using the midsection of your torso, bump uglies with the surrounding air. This may generate laughter, disgust—or possibly a date. All good options.

MEAN MUGGIN'

Our research has proven the effectiveness of placing your grill all up in the cups' business. Just beware of contracting ball-in-the-eye-socket syndrome while you're at it.

THE STEP-BACK

Stand completely still directly behind the rack while your opponent sets up and aims their shot. Right before they're about to shoot, take a step back to throw off their depth perception.

NUDITY DISTRACTIONS

THE BUDDHA RUB

This move involves exposing one's midsection and rubbing it in a circular motion with both hands. Its effectiveness is proportional to one's obesity and sweat level.

CRACK'S LEGAL

Skin might be the largest organ of the human body, but the butt is the funniest. And exposing it to your competition is just plain smart.

THE OTHER RACK

Unlike some sports, Beer Pong presents a level playing field for the genders. Especially when breasts are partially exposed on that field.

MONKEY BRAINS

Exposing your beans to your opponents is a difficult move that should be used with caution and—we beg you—restraint.

TEAM DISTRACTIONS

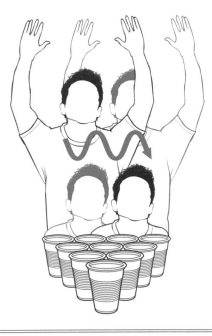

THE WAVE
Bring some of the excitement of the 1980s to your next game and let this repetitive movement lull your opponents into lazy shooting.

THE CONTINUOUS CHEST BUMP
If you have the stamina, this sternum-to-sternum move can be very effective. Be sure to stretch out beforehand, since pulling a hamstring while chest bumping is grounds for permanent embarrassment.

THE CIRQUE
Inspired by the guys in body paint and loin-cloths in Cirque du Soleil, you and your partner balance on top of each other. The skill thus displayed makes it impossible to ignore.

THE GANESHA
Named after the Hindu deity with an elephant's head and four arms. Stand directly behind your partner and alternate your arms up and down. This effect can be hypnotic—especially if your part-ner has an elephant's head.

ADVANCED TECHNIQUES

These advanced and controversial distractions require a bit of preparation in order to be executed properly.

THE FLASH BOMB

The player uses a small disposable camera—hidden at waist level—to produce a surprise distracting flash for opponents while they're in mid-throw. The two key words are "surprise" (timing is critical) and "disposable" (your camera might get smashed into pieces). As an added bonus, you could end up with some incriminating pictures for later use.

THE TALKING HEAD

Don't let those incriminating pictures of your opponents go to waste. Crop and enlarge the images so the faces fit on 8-by-11-inch pieces of paper. Print them out (preferably in color), trim the edges, and mount on sticks. Wave these head puppets right behind the cups. If you lose the match, the faces can be transferred to the closest dartboard.

THE WATERBOY

Under the guise of being a helpful player, you obsessively fill and refill the wash cups throughout the game. If your opponents accuse you of trying to throw them off their game, pretend to be hurt—you were only trying to be helpful, right?

THE STINK BALL

Literally, a very distasteful way to distract an opponent. After your opponents miss their shots, let the balls roll around on the floor a little bit. If it's an outdoor match, maybe let the ball take a stroll through the dirt. Then be sure to take a pass on giving it a bath in the water cup. Your opponent's gag reflex should be enough to distract them from playing any D.

THE CRANK CALL

This move perfectly blends skill and technology. Have your opponents' cell phone numbers at easy access on your phone. Just before they shoot, call their number.

THE DISTRACTION CONTROVERSY

. . . .

There's some debate regarding the role—and even the necessity—of distractions in Beer Pong. Here are three of the most common arguments for keeping on your own game.

1. **Distractions are an energy drain.**
    Jonathan Katz, a New York City—based clinical sports psychologist, stated in *Psychology Today* magazine: "Many athletes are putting time and energy into something that distracts them from playing their best. Playing well is the most intimidating factor." [Sep/Oct 1999]

2. **Distractions aren't sportsmanlike.**
    Some players who are fighting the good fight for Beer Pong respect see distractions as damaging to their cause. From their perspective, distraction techniques further separate the sport from other more "civilized" sports.

3. **Distractions can backfire.**
    When your competition sinks a shot despite your best distractions, it only fuels their flames. It can pump them up. And it can ultimately lead to their kicking your ass—literally and figuratively.

ALL-PRO QUOTE

When I shoot and I know I have to make the cup, most of the time I'm going to make that cup, and that's what separates me from someone who will use distractions during a game.

—NEIL GUERRIERO,
2007 World Series of Beer Pong Champion

Showmanship

Sure, placing the ball in the cup is how you win the game. But how you do it is what really matters. Finesse and style may not count for points, but they do count for something: entertainment.

Sport without entertainment is but mere hobby. The missing ingredient is showmanship—the sizzle on the steak of skill. But do not be fooled—bringing exhilaration and audience appeal to your game can be difficult for the uninitiated. To make it a little easier, we've created a top-level survey of the tactics that can be immediately implemented to spice up your game.

CELEBRATION

All sports talk about the thrill of victory. But few let it be expressed—and flaunted. Again, Beer Pong sets itself apart by embracing the need for emotional outbursts and allowing them to become part of the game itself. Consider the full spectrum of celebration options to provide the right level of intensity.

FIST MOVES

THE BUMP
An understated greeting used by jazz musicians, reggae artists, Stephen Colbert, and other people cooler than us.

THE PUMP
A more amplified single serving of celebration. Made famous by Tiger Woods, who is a popular player of a non–Beer Pong sport.

THE BALBOA

An enthusiastic, overhead double-fist pump—usually reserved for in-ring competition—it shows intensity to the world, and, more important, to the other team.

HIGH-FIVES

THE CLASSIC

The basic maneuver, with each person raising one hand to slap the raised hand of the other, is a simple yet effective way to punctuate just about any shot.

THE DOUBLE

All four hands are employed in this kicked-up-a-notch version, which should be used after impressive sinkage or minor victory.

THE DOUBLE DOWN-LOW

Also known as the May-Walsh Clap-Clap, this celebration begins as a double high-five and is followed by a double low-five. Ending it with a bikini-to-bikini full-body hug is purely optional.

ADVANCED CELEBRATION MOVES

THE WORM
The classic break-dancing move, in which the subject lies on the ground and moves his body in a rippling motion—much like a worm—is a guaranteed winner. Just make sure to avoid the pools of beer spillage collecting around the Beer Pong table.

THE CHASTAIN
In the throes of your emotional high, run across the floor, slide on your knees, and promptly remove your shirt. Style points if you are wearing a sports bra for this occasion; negative points if you are a guy.

THE DANCE OF JOY
Popularized by "Cousin Larry" and "Balki Bartokomous" of the TV sitcom *Perfect Strangers*. You and your teammate stand face to face with hands on each other's waist and shoulders. Then you perform a series of sideways leg kicks and jumps—ending with the "Cousin Larry" teammate being swept off his/her feet.

BEER PONG FACTOID

Both leads in *Perfect Strangers* (Mark Linn-Baker and Bronson Pichot) attended Yale University. It's not known if they played Beer Pong there.

THE CROTCH CHOP
This move was invented by professional wrestlers in the mid-1990s. To execute, raise your arms over your head in a "Y" formation. Bring your hands down in a "chop" motion, finishing right around crotch level. Consider adding the phrase "Suck it."

TRICK SHOTS IN THE GAME

There are few better ways to excite a crowd than with impressive trick shots. If made, any of these shots are guaranteed to increase the chances of pandemonium by at least 34 percent.

THE DOWNTOWN. Go back—way back—and make the shot from across the room. Other sports would give you three points for it. Beer Pong players trade in props, not points.

THE BABE RUTH. Call your shot, à la the Sultan of Swat, sink it, and then celebrate Bambino-style.

THE SMACK 'N' SHOT. Look your opponent in the eyes, talk some smack, and sink your shot without missing a beat.

THE AMBIDEXTROUS ASSASSIN. Switch to your opposite hand for the last shot—just because you can.

THE BEHIND-THE-BACK. A high degree of difficulty, yes, but a higher reward in reverence and adulation if you nail it.

THE EYES-CLOSED. The ultimate game closer, provided you avoid losing your balance and face-planting into the table.

THE LOOGIE. Place the ball in your mouth and forcefully spit it out, across the table, and hopefully into the cup.

THE SNIPER. Hit the cup in your opponent's hand. Even if it doesn't count for anything in some rules, it'll drive your opponents crazy—and make the crowd go wild.

THE SELF-SWAT. Bounce the ball at your end of the table. As it comes back up, use an open-handed swat to knock the ball across the table. For your opponents, this is the Beer Pong equivalent of being facialized by a slam dunk.

TRICK SHOTS OUTSIDE OF THE GAME

Freestyle shots can take a whole different form when performed outside of the game context. They're pure showboating, with no regard for the fundamentals of the game. Think of them as the streetball game of Beer Pong. The following are some of the basic tools of freestyle shooting.

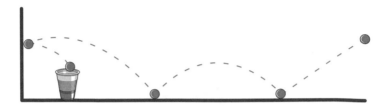

THE MULTIPLE BOUNCE

The bounce shot is a staple of Beer Pong. But bouncing the ball two, three, or four times—at a variety of angles and off a variety of surfaces—takes freestyling to a higher level.

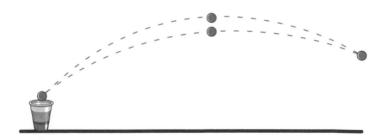

THE MULTIPLE-BALL SHOT

Make like a Harlem Globetrotter and knock down two shots with one toss.

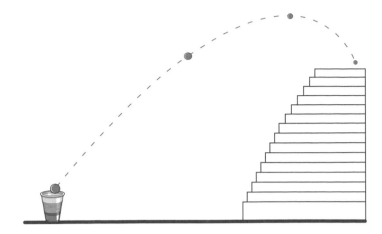

THE VERTIGO

Dropping the ball from dizzying heights adds a new dimension to a game that's usually played on a horizontal plane.

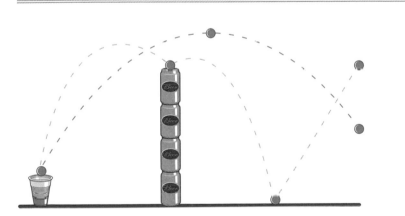

THE FOREIGN-OBJECT FINALE

Using obstacles to create barriers or unusual bouncing angles for your shot can separate it from the pack.

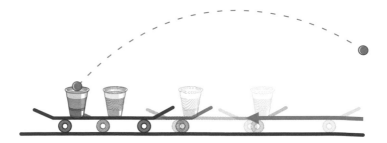

THE MOVING TARGET

Putting the cup in motion on an object such as a skateboard ratchets up the difficulty level. For a variation on this theme, set the shooter in motion. For example, shoot from a bicycle, escalator, or Pope-mobile.

HOW TO GAIN FREESTYLE FAME

We asked YouTube/MySpace Beer Pong trick-shot star and comedian "MarkBerry"—whose videos have been viewed millions of times online and even broadcast during the 2008 MLB All-Star Game—to share some of his tricks of the trade. Here's what he told us.

Keep it real.
No camera tricks. No strings attached. The Beer Pong community will study your shot like the Zapruder film; so don't try any funny stuff.

Use a wide and continuous shot.
Make sure the ball never leaves the frame, from the throw to the "money shot"— ball floating in the cup. This makes you less susceptible to claims that your shot was actually an editing trick.

Go big, then think small.
Don't settle for a quick, simple shot, because chances are it's been done before. Once you have the idea, then break it down to what could be possible.

Working

THE CROWD

Spectators make the sport. A crowd of cheering fans transforms a game into an event—a spectacle laced with tension, emotion, and adulation. But this excitement doesn't build itself. It takes work to work the crowd. And here's how.

In basketball, the crowd is considered the sixth man. In football, the home-field advantage is a significant factor in determining the game's outcome. In fact, spectator involvement is so important that it has spawned its own profession that employs thousands of undersized women and rhythmically gifted men: cheerleading. Here's how to harness the power of the crowd to elevate your game.

COACH SAYS

Win the crowd and you win the game. Unless you don't.

MAKE CONTACT.

Touch is the most basic of human needs. And you can use it to win the crowd—and the game. Try out one of the following variations to reach out.

THE VICTORY LAP

After your first win, make a lap around the table, high-fiving your soon-to-be fans along the way. If the crowd is more than one row deep, employ the two-hand multi-five approach. With this simple move, the foundation of a loyal crowd has been laid.

THE LAM-BEER LEAP

Inspired by the Green Bay Packers' signature leap-into-the-stands technique, this strategy involves your literally and physically being supported by the audience. Make sure you've appropriately engaged them before attempting it—a dive into an unprepared crowd could be sub-optimal.

THE SOUL TOUCH
More nuanced than the strategies above, this involves the repeated use of eye contact and knowing glances to keep individuals involved and win them over. A quick look and nod before a big shot says, "You, [name of person], and I are in this together."

MAKE DRAMA.
Like touch, the need to make sense of life's complexities through the construction of linear narratives is innate in all people. So use that, too. Here are some ways to bring more drama to your game:

THE DRAMATIC COMEBACK
The player-overcomes-adversity-and-wins storyline dominates sports history, from Kirk Gibson's walk-off homer in the 1988 World Series to Paul Lim's perfect dart game in the 1990 Embassy World Professional Darts Championship. Bring it into your repertoire. For example, pretend to injure your elbow, hobble off, accept sympathy from fans—and then return to finish the game.

THE EXTENDED ADDRESS
As in public speaking, a pregnant pause can build excitement and engagement. Before a critical shot, try taking a full minute to line up and focus your aim. Used strategically, and sparingly, this move will help get your audience to sit only on the edge portions of their seats.

THE CHEAP POP
In professional wrestling, this refers to blatantly pandering to local crowds and promising to "win one for the fans." So try invoking a local sports team, or simply try this: "Make some noise, [name of house/street/fraternity]!" An alternative version involves dedicating a shot to a person in the crowd who's injured or passed out.

MAKE MUSIC.

The ear canal is only 26 millimeters long. But it can carry a great deal of information directly to the heart. The careful application of music can be a powerful force in winning crowd support—and ultimately the game. Here are a few tips for getting it right:

ENLIVEN THE ATMOSPHERE
Release your inner DJ. Energizing the whole room with music creates a more engaged crowd. Look for songs with an upbeat tempo (*allegro* or *presto*) and a preponderance of beats or driving guitar.

STEAL THE HALO
This technique involves co-opting the positive associations inherent in the music for yourself. In other words, the good feeling elicited by the song creates a halo effect around you. To do this, become one with the song. Move your body to the rhythm. Sing the refrain if you are familiar with it.

FIND A SIGNATURE SONG
Finally, borrow a page from the once-popular sport of baseball, in which players choose their at-bat music. Arrange to have your song played when you first take the table for a game—and of course, after you inevitably win. This creates an "auditory logo" that your fans will come to recognize.

ALL-PRO QUOTE

When I play in big tournaments, I will use my iPod. I have specific songs I like to listen to depending on how important the game I'm playing in is, but I'm not going to give those out. Listen to whatever helps you hit cups. All I care about is hitting cups and winning the game.

—NEIL GUERRIERO,
2007 World Series of Beer Pong Champion

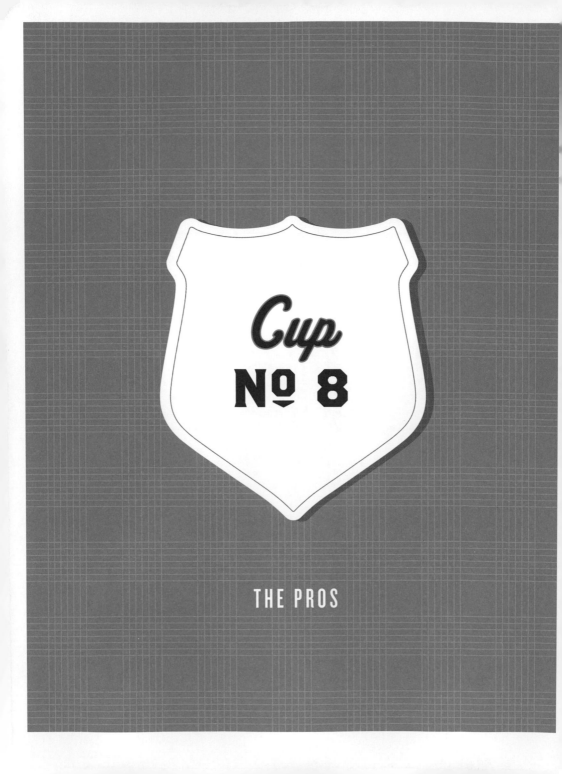

Cup
№ 8

THE PROS

THE ABUNDANCE OF PROFESSIONAL LEVELS REMOVES ANY DOUBT OF BEER PONG'S SPORTING LEGITIMACY.

BEER PONG OFFERS A PLETHORA of chances to bring your game to the majors: thousands of local affiliations, scores of regional organizations, and several national and international events. With ever-increasing cash prizes and a rising level of competition, Beer Pong is on track to join the ranks of such sports as basketball, hot-dog eating, and poker, which are not only sources of entertainment and profit but also outlets for us to channel our hunger for competition.

In order to attain the highest level of the sport and, perhaps more important, attain bragging rights, one must undergo a transformation—a series of steps to go from "regular Joe" to fulltime pro. We've laid out those steps for you here, and explain what you can expect when you make it to the pro level. But it will take more that just reading a book to become a pro. You'll need to hone your skills, face competitors under extreme pressure, and commit to the goal with the intensity of Clark Griswold leading his family to Wally World.

Admittedly, this is not the path for every player. There are some individuals who are content with recreational Beer Pong—playing for fun, camaraderie, and other intangible benefits. And we respect those players. But the sport's growth requires other players to strive for more—to dream of fame, fortune, and obsessive fan stalkers. These are the heroes and heroines who will shape the history of sport. And they will be the ones to first reap the rewards of being pioneers.

So after you read this chapter, we ask that you pose this one question to yourself: "Am I ready to go pro?"

Step 1

NAME YOUR TEAM

Few sports allow the players themselves to decide on the team name. After all, a name provides a first impression, a competitive edge, and a collective identity across the sporting world. In short, it's not to be taken lightly.

But as you have read, Beer Pong is different than other sports. The democratic, decentralized gestalt of its structure—and at the heart of its very ethos—places the power in the hands of the participants. And with that power comes great responsibility: Your team name can't blow.

Choosing a team name is often the first step in conveying the essence of you and your teammate. It's your brand, which communicates a powerful combination of denotations and connotations to your competitors, spectators, and the adoring public. So choose wisely. To support you in this process, we've provided several proven approaches for choosing the best name to take your game to the pros.

▷ Be as hardcore and aggressive as possible. Give your team the best competitive advantage with a name that strikes fear in the hearts of the other team.
   EXAMPLES: *The Cup Crushers, the Ball Bashers, the Eliminators, the Two Horsemen of the A-PONG-calypse*

COACH SAYS

Naming your team is like choosing a tattoo. You need to worry about what it will look like in 50 years.

▷ Boast of your team's skills. Sure, you need to walk the walk, but don't overlook the importance of talking the talk.
   EXAMPLES: *The Sharp Shooters, Lone Wolves, Sure Shot and the Bring-Backs, Team Sink*

▷ Show your veteran status. The mere fact that you have played for many years and weathered many a game tells other teams you've been there and sunk that.

   EXAMPLES: *The '79 Bombers, the Lehigh Beirut Club, the Schlitz Pongers, Team McCain*

▷ Use reverse psychology. The game in the mind is as important as the game on the table. So fool your opponents into underestimating your skills before unleashing a torrent of awesomeness upon them.

   EXAMPLES: *The Pretty Pongers, Team Choke, the Blue Balls, First-Time Tossers, Team You'll Probably Beat*

▷ Incorporate your geographic identity. As a nod to the customs of older, traditional sports, use your location to inspire your name and, with any luck, to rally local support.

   EXAMPLES: *The Springfield Sinkers, the Richmond Ringers, Scranton's Finest, Team [insert area code] All-Stars*

▷ Degrade the other team. Humility may get you friends, but it won't get you the sweet taste of victory.

   EXAMPLES: *Team Game Over, Team Your Mom, Team Taste Our Balls, Deez Nuts, and the You Might As Well Just Go Homes.*

▷ Take the easy route. If all else fails, throw the word "Team" in front of another word or words.

   EXAMPLES: *Team Players, Team Balls, Team Redhead, Team Barry, Team No Creativity*

THE DO'S AND DON'TS OF ESTABLISHING YOUR TEAM NAME

....

DO be consistent in using it. If your short-term memory is shot, write it down early in the evening.

DO publicly stake a claim to your trademark. In other words, the team with its name emblazoned loudly on its shirts has rights over any others.

DO avoid common names that are too widespread to establish ownership. These include "The Ballers," "Balls Deep," and any variation of a name involving "Ballz."

DON'T be too graphic or offensive. While fun that first night, these names don't respond well to the light of day—or to possible merchandising contracts. These include the @#*! Punchers," "The Sheep ?@*&%s," and "The $#!@ing #?*@! %#&*s".

100 Certified-Awesome Names

We've compiled a list of fully screened and filtered potential Beer Pong team names. Feel free to adopt any of them for your own team.

1. Team We Own You
2. Fightin' Whiteys
3. 12 Ounces of Freedom
4. Everyone Can Shut the Hell Up
5. Huey Lewis & the Brews
6. Chug Life
7. Chicko's Bail Bonds
8. Team Speaker City
9. Ball in the Family
10. Cleveland Steamers
11. The Ted Kennedys
12. Los Lobbers
13. The Ball Grabbers
14. Beer's Looking at You
15. A Beer in the Headlights
16. The Fightin' Amish
17. The Tea Baggers
18. Beer and Present Danger
19. Beer as Folk
20. The Sarasota Saucers
21. The Ball Busters
22. The Donkey Punchers
23. Beer Eye for the Straight Guy
24. Cup Fever
25. The Drunk Dialers
26. The Table Dancers
27. The Dixie Cups
28. The Blue Flames
29. Uncle Jesse's House of Awesomeness
30. The Old 86ers
31. Rack of Ages
32. Victorious Secrets
33. Team Score-gasm
34. The Gotham Knights
35. Just Here for the Beer
36. Brew Kids on the Block
37. Mob Barley & The Ballers
38. Everyone Gets Laid
39. Foul Balls
40. The Matzo Ballers
41. Two the Hard Way
42. Van Hagar
43. O-Face
44. Curious George's Balls
45. The Stereotypical Mafia References
46. We're Gonna Dip Our Balls in It!
47. Team America
48. The Blooper Reel
49. The Clown Punchers

In the quest to become a champion, one must transform from a casual player of a sport into a true athlete. And part of this transformation is the symbolic application of a uniform.

Transcending mere clothing, a uniform signals the subjugation of the individual to the team. Wearing a truly awful jersey can be a humbling and team-building experience—just ask any member of the 1982 Astros. In addition, it marks one's complete immersion in the sport.

When considering the many options for one's sartorial selection, we recommend taking the following criteria into consideration:

▷ **ERGONOMICS.** First and foremost, the uniform must allow a full range of movement in both the upper and lower extremities. Your throwing arm needs to be unhindered, making bulky or clingy uniforms a no-no.

▷ **BODY TEMPERATURE.** To focus 100 percent on game play, you must be comfortable in any location. In other words, dress in layers—with one layer being underpants.

▷ **PRESENCE.** If a uniform is unveiled and no one notices it, did it really ever exist? Philosophical questions aside, you need to strive to draw attention to your team.

▷ **WASHABILITY.** Due to the plethora of fluids (beer, dirty water, saliva) and locations (basements, fraternity houses, dorms) involved in the sport, the uniform must hold up to multiple launderings.

▷ **COVERAGE.** Please consult your state and local decency laws.

UNIFORM CATEGORIES

ATHLETICS-BASED UNIFORMS

These are the most obvious choice for players who take the sport seriously and are in it to win it ("it" being nothing short of total domination).

EXAMPLES: *Golf shirts, baseball shirts, mess football shirts, cycling jerseys*

PROS: Take full advantage of the technology and research invested in the clothing for more traditional sports.

CONS: Can be expensive, depending on items purchased; ubiquity limits their impact; some versions (e.g., cycling jerseys) accentuate love handles.

SPONSORED UNIFORMS

For entrepreneurial players, these uniforms offer the perfect combination of coverage and commerce.

EXAMPLES: *A T-shirt with a logo (or logos) on it*

PROS: Sponsorship revenue helps defray the costs of professional play; intimidating to competitors who assume that only skilled teams get backers.

CONS: Large prominent silk-screened logos can limit breathability; possible conflicts of interest if you use a competitive company's services or hot wings.

DISTRACTION-BASED UNIFORMS

Designed for one express purpose, these are all form, no function. Wearing one is a calculated risk that might just pay off in victory.

EXAMPLES: *Diapers, togas, hula skirts with coconut bras (on guys), low-cut anything (on women)*

PROS: Brings an unfair advantage to the table and can cement a team's reputation/notoriety.

CONS: Embarrassment, humiliation, incriminating pictures that may end future political aspirations, coconut chafing.

HOW TO GET A SPONSOR FOR YOUR TEAM

It's a dream of many players to get a company to literally put their money where your mouth is. But it doesn't have to be a pipe dream. Here are several tips for getting your skills to pay the bills.

1. Commit to a schedule. A sponsor is buying the exposure of their brand. You need to show them you'll be getting them visibility at a guaranteed number of events.
2. Reach a bigger audience. Tell the company how you will amplify its message by seeking PR, creating viral online videos, and making public appearances. Figure out how to do it later.
3. Prime the promotional pump. Take a cue from NASCAR and offer a variety of sponsorship opportunities. Consider giving away some smaller ones to show a bigger company that you are a credible investment.
4. Use PowerPoint. This Microsoft product produces a Pavlovian response in marketers. Use pie charts and the word "synergies" to make your pitch irresistible.

Step 3

JOIN A LEAGUE

Are you ready to see how your game stacks up against the world of competition beyond the four walls of your apartment? A league is the perfect opportunity to develop your game, bond with your partner, and build the competitive edge you need to be a champion.

At this stage in the Beer Pong life cycle, all leagues are regional organizations that host formalized recurring game nights. For aspiring Beer Pong professionals, they offer several important benefits:

▷ More games against more teams. Beating your brother and his friend Tube-sock Tony week after week will not take you to the majors. Leagues offer opportunities to face off against a wide variety of strong competitors. This is the only way to sharpen your skills.

▷ A way to track your statistical progress. By virtue of the fact that teams play in an organized—and recordable—fashion, leagues provide an opportunity to go beyond simple wins and losses. Understanding your game from a variety of statistical perspectives allows you to understand your strengths and weaknesses.

▷ Bonding. With all of the competition and quest for greatness, it's sometimes easy to forget that Beer Pong offers an opportunity for camaraderie and bonding. Leagues offer this in spades. By thier very nature, they allow players to get together and have a good time.

Now that you understand why you should join a league, you'll need to find one. Due to the fact they're popping up all the time, a quick search of the Internet could help you locate a league in your region. To further support your quest, we've cataloged some of the most-established leagues across the country.

COACH SAYS

If you don't challenge yourself by moving up in competition, you can't expect to improve. And if you don't improve, then why the hell are you reading a book about this sport? Seriously, someone explain that to me.

LEAGUE NAME: Maryland Beer Pong
FOUNDED: January 2005, by Austin Lanham and Jim Reiter
AREA: Northeast—Baltimore and Washington, D.C., plus surrounding suburbs
MEMBERS: 900+
MEETS: Once a week, with four leagues a year and state championship main event
WHY: "We wanted to bring together the best Beer Pong competition, have fun with it, and see where it would go. When we started, there wasn't anything like what we were trying to do, so we kind of invented the organized Beer Pong league."
WEBSITE: www.mdbeerpong.com

LEAGUE NAME: Boston Beer Pong
FOUNDED: February 2005, by Marc Musco, Brian Flynn, and Dean Brassington
AREA: Northeast—Boston and the South Shore
MEMBERS: 80+
MEETS: Once a week
WHY: "We were talking about how fun it would be to be able to go to a bar and play in a Beer Pong tournament—not to mention the free beer and ladies that come along with it. That began the process of what is now Boston Beer Pong."
WEBSITE: www.myspace.com/beerpongofboston

MARYLAND BEER PONG: A SUCCESS STORY

●●●●●●●●●●●●●●●●

Austin and Jim Reiter started Maryland Beer Pong, one of the oldest and largest Beer Pong league in the world, in January 2005. The first challenge they had to overcome was getting venues to agree to host their events. At the time, Beer Pong at bars was rare. They tried to sell a mutually beneficial scenario, where the bars got good business and the players got a quality event, and they succeeded. Once they got local bars involved, the owners saw the potential and embraced their events. After that, they were able to start looking for better and better venues.

The second challenge they faced was getting players to join their leagues. They used guerilla-style marketing to promote their league by hitting the streets and handing out promo cards at local bars and at major Maryland sporting events such as the Preakness horse race. In the beginning, they had a lot of time between events, so they were able to hang up fliers and promote their league. Austin and Jim worked hard to run professional and quality events so they could build a following. Once they succeeded, finding players was not a problem.

The final challenge was creating the model for a successful Beer Pong association. There was nothing like this at the time, so they were basically developing a model that most leagues around the country now use today. They discovered that weekly leagues were a great way for teams to improve, since they could play many games against good competition. Now, Maryland Beer Pong is considered by many to be the largest and best league in the country.

BEER PONG FACTOID

CNY Beer Pong was the first league to use non-alcoholic liquid in its cups. Now every league in the nation is following its lead.

LEAGUE NAME: CNY Beer Pong
FOUNDED: January 2006, by Jason N. Hughes
AREA: Northeast—Syracuse, New York
MEMBERS: 500+
MEETS: Once a month
WHY: "Where else can one find this bond that our parents and grandparents were so lucky to have? The Beer Pong league! Now men and women can be a part of something that centers on socializing and making friends!"
WEBSITE: www.cnybeerpong.com

College House Beer Pong League

LEAGUE NAME: College House Beer Pong League (CHBPL)
FOUNDED: September 2003, by Brodey Callies
AREA: Midwest—Milwaukee and Appleton, Wisconsin
MEMBERS: 200+
MEETS: Once a week
WHY: "Well, the winters are pretty cold here in this city."
WEBSITE: www.chbpl.com

LEAGUE NAME: Clutch Pong
FOUNDED: October 2007, by Tim Mentink
AREA: Midwest—Michigan: Jackson, Lansing, Ann Arbor, Auburn Hills, Grand Rapids, Mt. Pleasant, Flint, Kalamazoo
MEMBERS: 200+
MEETS: Once a month.
WHY: "Seeing a void in the Midwest Beer Pong scene and knowing we have some of the best Beer Pong players in the world, we decided to take a shot in the dark and try something to get people around the Midwest motivated and pumped to come out."
WEBSITE: www.clutchpong.com

LEAGUE NAME: Michigan Pong League
FOUNDED: February 2008, by Nick Velissaris
AREA: Midwest—Ann Arbor, Michigan
MEMBERS: Varies
MEETS: Once a week
WHY: "Our main goal is to unify the good Michigan players."
WEBSITE: www.tripletowin.com

NEW MEXICO BEER PONG LEAGUE

LEAGUE NAME: New Mexico Beer Pong League
FOUNDED: May 2006
FOUNDED BY: Amber Morales
AREA: Southwest—Carlsbad and Las Cruces, New Mexico; El Paso, Texas
MEMBERS: 60+
MEETS: Every other week
WHY: "We wanted to do something that no one around here was doing, and we were tired of hearing, 'There's nothing to do, we need something new.' So we decided, since we all love Beer Pong, why not start a league and we could all get together and have a blast."
WEBSITE: www.myspace.com/nmbeerpong21

LEAGUE NAME: San Antonio Pong League (SAPL)
FOUNDED: April 2008, by Rick Odom and Darryl Blanton
AREA: Southwest—Texas: San Antonio, Corpus Christi, San Marcus, Austin
MEMBERS: 100+
MEETS: Five nights a week
WHY: "We made friends with a guy from New York who showed us how to play, and we saw how well everyone got along while playing. It was just a complete good time full of laughs and friendship, so we decided to start our own league down here to spread the fun."
WEBSITE: www.myspace.com/sanantoniopongleague

LEAGUE NAME: Southern California Beer Pong (SCBP)
FOUNDED: March 2007, by Peter Rusch and Tyler Green
AREA: West Coast—California: San Diego, El Segundo, West LA, and Hollywood
MEMBERS: 80+
MEETS: Once a week
WHY: "We wanted to promote the sport of Beer Pong and bring together the community of players we knew existed. We started with a few open tournaments, giving away cash prizes, but we also wanted the more communal feel of teams playing each other week after week. League play is less cutthroat than tournament games, as everyone gets to play the same number of games whether they win or lose."
WEBSITE: www.socalbeerpong.com

LEAGUE NAME: San Diego Beer Pong League
FOUNDED: December 2007, by Casey Webster and Ronny Rader
AREA: West Coast—San Diego
MEMBERS: 100+
MEETS: Twice a week
WHY: "A friend opened a new bar in San Diego and needed a way to get people in. Beer Pong was a no-brainer!"
WEBSITE: www.sdbeerpong.com

LEAGUE NAME: Central California Beer Pong
FOUNDED: March 2006, by Eric Welch
AREA: West Coast—Fresno, California
MEMBERS: 125+
MEETS: Varies
WHY: "A lot of it is because people enjoy Beer Pong and the dynamics of the game. Beer Pong is a fascinating combination of social interaction and competition that makes for a unique experience for participants."
WEBSITE: www.centralcalbeerpong.com

LOOKING TO START A LEAGUE?

••••••••••••••

Austin Lanham of Maryland Beer Pong offers this advice to those looking to start their own league:

1. **Find a bar.** You have to find a bar willing to work with you. The only way a league will work is if the space is conducive to play and if the price is affordable.

2. **Promote.** You need to work hard promoting the league. Everyone you talk to will seem interested and say they'll join. When it comes down to it, it's harder to get people to actually show up.

3. **Start small.** You are not going to be able to run huge leagues right off the bat. Don't make promises to bars and players that you can't keep.

LEAGUE NAME: Sink It Premiership
FOUNDED: February 2008, by Joey Danelo and Brent Weber
AREA: West Coast— San Pedro, California
MEMBERS: 40+
MEETS: Once a week
WHY: "Everyone in the league knew each other and hung out several times a week anyway, so we found a venue that would allow us all to get together at the same time, have some tenacious competition, and prepare us for the tournaments later in the year."
WEBSITE: www.sinkitpremiership.com

Step 4

PLAY IN A TOURNAMENT

The recreational game is how many players have fallen in love with the sport. But the tournament is the next step in competitiveness. It gives winning and losing true consequences—and rewards.

If you are happy just playing for fun, we encourage you to continue your hobby. Because once you get a taste of the intoxicating rush of adrenaline as you climb to the dizzying heights of a tournament bracket, you might get hooked.

Of course, in addition to the quenching of latent bloodlust, tournament play can help benefit your game in several other ways:

▷ **SKILLS UNDER PRESSURE.** A tournament is the perfect chance to see how your skills hold up to pressure from cutthroat competition and an unforgiving format, where elimination lurks behind every cup.

▷ **VARIETY OF COMPETITION.** There is no better way to see where you rank than to expose your skills to the most diverse group of opponents.

▷ **VARIETY OF COMPENSATION.** Tournaments offer something more than just bragging rights: cold hard cash. Sometimes a few hundreds dollars, sometimes many more.

Now, the only thing to do is locate a tournament. Here are a few places to look:

▷ **BARS.** The most common and most accessible location is your local watering hole. Most bars that host Beer Pong nights aren't shy about it, so keep a lookout for posters and flyers.

▷ **EVENT LISTINGS.** Organizations from fraternities to charities host tournaments to raise money for a good cause—or just more beer. If you are interested, inquire about whether an event is open to the public.

▷ **THE MAJORS.** These are tournaments with a capital "T." Some are under the auspices of a league. Others are autonomous enterprises. All represent the big time. Later in this chapter, we'll take a look at two of the biggest: The World Beer Pong Tour and The World Series of Beer Pong.

The Statistics of the Game:
BEYOND THE WINS AND LOSSES

KEEPING STATS IS ESSENTIAL to taking your Beer Pong game to the next level. The most basic statistics, such as shooting percentage, can be tracked with pen and paper. While this may smack of homework and geekdom, it's actually as fun as scanning the box score of your favorite sports team. The easiest method is to stand tableside and keep track of hits and misses. This location will also give you an excellent opportunity to mock players who are shooting below the Mendoza line.

After the game, enter the numbers in a spreadsheet, and you'll have plenty of statistics to pore over Bill James–style. To take it to the next level, keep track of these same stats based on the opponents you play against and the venue you are playing in. You may find that you shoot 50 percent against one team, but a mere 20 percent against another. Or you may be a great player in the comforting confines of your home table but crumble in hostile road environments.

While basic stats can be tracked easily with pen and paper or a spreadsheet, more advanced stats can be recorded through programs like PongTracker.com. This site allows you to record each shot and then view reports on a large array of stats, including shooting percentages for each rack type. Shooting percentages by rack will show you who the real sharpshooters are and who can be counted on to hit the last cup, versus the chumps that are only good when the rack is full.

In our humble opinion, the most important Beer Pong statistical categories are:

1. PERSONAL WINNING PERCENTAGE

BEST-CASE SCENARIO: You are the '27 Yankees.
WORST-CASE SCENARIO: You are the '62 Mets.
HOW IT CAN HELP: Provides a clear picture of where you stand in the Beer Pong hierarchy.

2. TEAM WINNING PERCENTAGE

BEST-CASE SCENARIO: You are as good or better with a partner.
WORST-CASE SCENARIO: Adding a teammate causes your win rate to plummet.
HOW IT CAN HELP: Lets you know if you need to find a new partner ASAP or mask the fact that your teammate is carrying your ass.

3. SHOOTING PERCENTAGE ON THE FINAL CUP

BEST-CASE SCENARIO: When the game's on the line, you are like Jordan, Montana, and Jeter rolled into one.
WORST-CASE SCENARIO: You stink like skunked beer when it comes to putting the game away.
HOW IT CAN HELP: Exposes any mental deficiencies in your game.

4. OVERALL SHOOTING PERCENTAGE

BEST-CASE SCENARIO: Your game is akin to Larry Legend's.
WORST-CASE SCENARIO: You might as well be aiming for the floor.
HOW IT CAN HELP: Gives you a snapshot of your overall game.

5. SHOOTING PERCENTAGE ON SPECIFIC RACKS

BEST-CASE SCENARIO: Your percentage barely changes from rack to rack.
WORST-CASE SCENARIO: You couldn't hit the 1-3 split from two feet out if the game depended on it (and it probably has).
HOW IT CAN HELP: Focuses you on problem spots you should work on.

HOW TO THROW YOUR OWN TOURNAMENT

If you are having trouble entering a tournament—or have an entrepreneurial streak—the solution is simple: Host your own. Here's how.

1. PICK THE VENUE. Make sure to secure a location that's big enough to accommodate the players, spectators, and members of the press.

2. FULLY SUPPLY THE GOODS. Be prepared to run multiple tables at the same time—with an eye toward rearranging things to have the finals in the most dramatic position as possible.

3. COLLECT THE CASH. Make the prize amounts clear, as well as any tournament administration fees. Then shake everyone down for the money.

4. DETERMINE THE FORMAT. One option is a simple single-elimination bracket in which a team is automatically out of the event after one loss. A more preferable, and often used, format is a double-elimination tournament, which requires a team to lose twice.

5. POST THE RULES UP FRONT. Nothing sidetracks good tournament mojo like claims of cheating or misinterpretation of the rules.

6. AWARD PRIZES. Don't let victory go unrewarded. Hold a ceremony and present a trophy along with the cash. Also, give out secondary prizes for other achievements—or dubious achievements.

THE WORLD BEER PONG TOUR

The World Beer Pong Tour was founded by Peter Altholz and Sam Pines in August 2006. They packed an SUV with tons of cups, balls, and collapsible tables and traveled to six cities in New York to host Beer Pong tournaments. After coming back to their hometown tired and worn out, they realized their destiny, and the World Beer Pong Tour was born.

Now they're running three tours covering 35 major cities and college towns across 11 states, with three touring vehicles and a full-time staff. Having hosted more than 85 events since the tour's inception, thcsc guys have given away more than $120,000 in cash and prizes—including trips to Jamaica, Las Vegas, and Cancun.

The World Beer Pong Tour is the biggest tour in the Beer Pong universe. Its organizers are striving to bring Beer Pong into the mainstream by promoting it as a sport instead of a "drinking game." At all of their tournaments, drinking is 100 percent optional, and players are always offered the choice to play with water if they prefer. By promoting good sportsmanship, camaraderie, and good-natured competition, the tour is helping grow the sport in new ways.

For more information or to join the tour, check out www.worldpongtour.com.

START YOUR OWN TOUR DE PONG

··················

Peter Altholz, president of the World Beer Pong Tour, offers this advice for running a successful tour.

1. **Be ambitious.** Don't let anyone tell you that the road to success is a 9-5 while you're working your way up the corporate ladder. Put yourself out there and do things that people thought were impossible.
2. **Check the law.** Different states and municipalities have different laws regarding playing games in bars. In some places, you can't play with beer in the cups (only water), so learn the law before you set out to host a tournament.
3. **Get sponsored.** Most businesses are looking to build partnerships, as long as they benefit both sides. Make it worth a company's while and you could end up with free merchandise for prizes, or more.

THE WORLD SERIES OF BEER PONG

This is the tournament of all tournaments. For the true Beer Pong player, there is no pinnacle of competition higher than the World Series of Beer Pong. The glory and grandeur of the sport's biggest stage has been the source of some of Beer Pong's greatest moments—and also its most heartbreaking disappointments. The huge cash prize and the intensity of the competition at the World Series of Beer Pong brings out true character like no other spectacle.

Founders Duncan Carroll and Billy Gaines are dedicated to elevating the sport to new heights—and new levels of legitimacy. Their mission is to diminish the potential negative aspects of Beer Pong so players can focus on the positive characteristics of the game: the competition, the socialization, the good times.

The growing popularity of Beer Pong necessitated a national event. This three-day competitive extravaganza is held once a year in Las Vegas. It started with a $10,000 prize in 2005; today it draws more than 1,000 players from the U.S. and abroad, who compete for the chance to win a $50,000 purse.

BEER PONG FACTOID

Past Champions of the World Series of Beer Pong

2006: Team France
Nicholas Velissaris and Jason Coben (Michigan)

2007: We Own Your Face
Neil Guerriero and Antonio Vassilatos
(New York)

2008: Chauffeuring the Fat Kid
Jeremy Hughes and Michael Orr (California)

2009: Smashing Time
Mike Popielarski and Ron Hamilton (New York)

HERE'S SOME ADVICE FROM DUNCAN AND BILLY ON HOSTING A TOURNAMENT.

....

1. **Make a pitch.** The more customers a bar has on a given night, the more money it will presumably make. So find out what days and times a bar doesn't have a lot of customers, and then tell the bar that you can use your ability to leverage Beer Pong to draw more customers to the bar during those off-peak times.

2. **Ask what the bar can do for you.** You should definitely brainstorm incentives that would make a bar want a ton of Beer Pong players there, but don't forget to see what the bar can do for you. For example, bars often have their own means of marketing themselves and their events. Thus, they may be willing to include your event on fliers, on their website, or in radio ads.

3. **Discuss distributors.** The bar may be able to talk local distributors into hooking up with some deals. For example, the bar may be willing to give discounted beer to participants or to provide general drink specials that enhance the overall perceived value of your event.

4. **Get the word out.** Don't misrepresent what you are offering, and don't be an idiot and just expect people to show up. One easy way to get some exposure for your event is to run some open tables with unorganized pickup games in the bar for a few nights over the weeks prior to your event. This will help get people interested in the game, let them know the bar has Beer Pong on certain nights, and give you a chance to tell people about the real event you have coming up.

And unlike other World Series in sports, it's still possible for players like you to purchase entry into the World Series of Beer Pong. The WSOBP Satellite network allows players to earn a slot by winning a local tournament. These tournaments have developed into a great way for players to gauge local competition and also a great way for some players to earn serious money.

For more information or to sign up for the next World Series of Beer Pong, check out www.bpong.com.

Step 5

MAKE BEER PONG
AN OLYMPIC EVENT

As you can see, Beer Pong has it all: leagues, tours, and even a World Series. What's missing? The international stage and unparalleled pageantry that is the Olympics.

The brutal reality is that not many of us are strong enough to be a weightlifter or Swedish enough to be a cross-country skier. Fortunately, Beer Pong can be our collective answer for striking Olympic gold. To make it an Olympic sport, we, the community of Beer Pong enthusiasts, just have to follow the steps below:

OLYMPIC SPORTS THAT SHOULD BE REMOVED TO MAKE WAY FOR BEER PONG

••••••••••••••••

BIATHLON. So dull even the inclusion of firearms can't make it cool.
THE 10K WALK. Where's Ashton? The sports world's been Punk'd for decades now.
CURLING. Combines the exhilaration of sweeping with the excitement of frostbite.
TABLE TENNIS. Isn't regular tennis enough? (There's not ice *and* air hockey, after all.) Just leave the tables and balls—we'll put them to good use.

▷ **DEVELOP A FOLLOWING.** An Olympic event must be practiced by men in at least 75 countries and four continents, and by women in at least 40 countries and three continents. Done, and done.

▷ **CREATE A GOVERNING BODY.** The sport must be regulated by an international federation. We're working on it, okay?

▷ **SUBMIT A PROPOSAL.** The federation also must file a highly involved application with the International Olympic Committee. This smacks of homework.

▷ **PARTICIPATE AS A DEMONSTRATION SPORT.** If the IOC is impressed with the federation's application, the event will then be welcomed to participate as . . . Actually, let's just let the Olympic officials beg, with torch in hand, to include a little thing called the greatest sport ever invented. Take that.

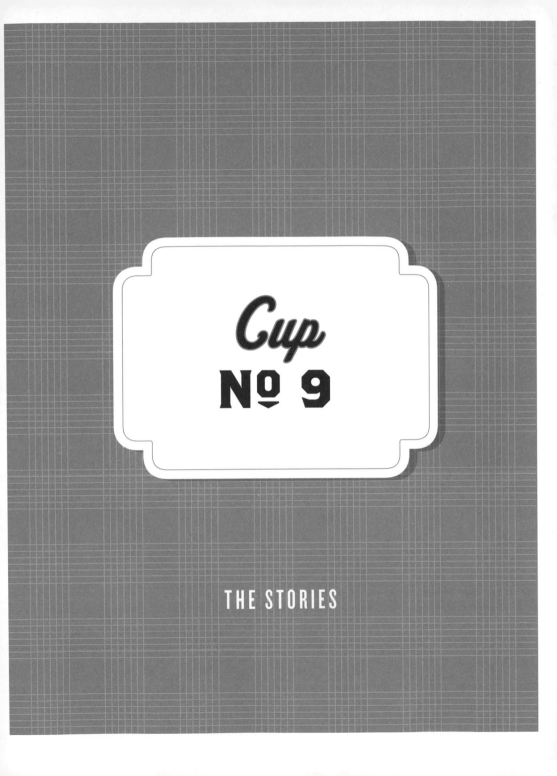

Cup
№ 9

THE STORIES

IT'S TIME TO LEARN FROM THE PLAYERS WHO ARE ON— BUT WITH THEIR ELBOWS BEHIND—THE FRONT LINES OF THE SPORT.

AS A NASCENT SPORT, Beer Pong lacks the long tradition of sports journalism like that devoted to other athletic pursuits. Sports like baseball and football have media infrastructures that have been built over generations—and employed thousands of chubby ex-players and skinny statisticians.

But it is only fitting that the narratives of a sport as democratic as Beer Pong are captured and shared in a similarly democratic manner. The citizen journalists of the Beer Pong community do not report to an editor-in-chief. They do not stick to AP standards. Or, in some cases, do they even bother much with verisimilitude.

But report they do.

Social media like Facebook, MySpace, and even an offline network called "People Talking to People" are prime channels for the distribution of Beer Pong narratives. Tales of great victories, crushing defeats, and unexpected opponents are dispersed into the culture at large. And with each one, the history of the sport—and its foundation of awesomeness—is built, one tale at a time.

We believe this process is critical for the further establishment of Beer Pong as a mainstay of American sports culture. So in order to encourage this practice, we've pulled together a sampling of stories to share with you, the fine readers of this book and pioneers of this sport. We hope they will inspire you to preserve your tales of the table, too.

Players Get Played

For those who remain unconvinced that Beer Pong is the great equalizer among sports, this tale should remove all doubts.

We were out at a bar in New York City on one of their famous Beer Pong nights. With two dominating wins under our belts, my roommate and I sized up the next round of "victims."

This third match of Beer Pong would solidify our dynasty. Two unassuming girls came to the table with the refilled pitcher. They looked like twins—home-schooled, physics-club-joining, unicorn-statue-collecting twins.

"Cakewalk," we thought. There was no way this pair was going to beat us. My roommate and I both played basketball in college. These two looked like they had never even attended a basketball game.

Mark it down as a "W." With the crowded bar gathered around, I gave my roommate his Ping-Pong ball and took my first shot.

Game over—but not the way we expected.

They literally hit two back-to-back shots, and before we knew it, we had lost. Smoked, really. We got played. I'd say they got lucky—but winning by eight cups is hard to excuse. We didn't get to play again that night.

Next time, I wanna see some ID.

—Matt Zalewski

ALL-PRO QUOTE

Beer Pong is the great equalizer. The biggest dude in the world could lose to an 85-pound girl with a steady hand.

And it's awesome to see them cry when they do.

—STEVE HOFSTETTER
Comedian and sports radio personality

Why Beer Pong Should Be Televised

Storytelling is an art form that can be expressed in a variety of media, and when it comes to sports, video is the strongest of all. Anyone who has watched a sporting event on television knows that it can build the tension, heighten the drama, and strengthen one's love for the game. With that in mind, here are some reasons why Beer Pong should be televised.

1. **PREGAME BUILDUPS.** Televised Beer Pong would allow programmers to build captivating pregame storylines for the fans at home. For example, a scrappy team of misfits is pitted against an inspiring black guy/white guy tandem of cops—who are just one day from retirement.

2. **INSTANT REPLAY.** Imagine getting a chance to better scrutinize a brilliant bounce shot or a perfectly executed fundamental again—and from multiple angles. Envision a Beer Pong color analyst using a telestrator or "pong-estrator" to further break down a player's table positioning or shooting technique. And when a streaker hurdles the table in midgame for airtime, we need to see that again.

3. **WAGERING.** Beer Pong tournaments are ideally suited for amateur bracket pools—like NCAA's March Madness—creating excitement at local pubs and significantly decreasing worker productivity at the office.

4. **IT'S BETTER THAN WHAT'S ON NOW.** Who wouldn't much rather watch Beer Pong than what's currently offered? The range of emotions and the story arc of a Beer Pong match easily top even the most scripted of "reality" TV shows.

5. **THE SPORTS-BAR MILIEU.** Hot wings. Cute waitresses. Fan camaraderie. Beer Pong on plasmas. It's seamless.

by Christopher Barish, author of *The Armchair Quarterback Playbook: The Ultimate Guide to Watching Football*.

Championship Thrills

The winners of the third World Series of Beer Pong tell the story of their dramatic victory.

After we won our semifinals match at the World Series of Beer Pong III and realized we were going to be playing in the championship, we were phenomenally pumped. The pressure of playing a game for $50,000 was intense. We were ready, though. We had been playing the entire latter part of our lives for this and couldn't appreciate the opportunity any more than we did at that moment.

We knew the two gentlemen we were about to play—the Iron Wizard Coalition (IWC)—were superb throwers. They had placed a sound beating on us earlier that day to put us into the loser's bracket, meaning we had to win two games and they needed only one. They were scruffy-looking bearded men but showed sportsmanship and cordiality similar to that of Olympic athletes. The four of us shook hands, cracked a joke or two, had a laugh, wished each other good luck, and took our respective sides of the fabled championship table.

And so it began. We quickly lost ground as the IWC came out firing. I don't know if it was the excitement, the lack of sleep, the pressure, or the fatigue, but we weren't shooting like we knew we could—and had to. Before we knew it, the IWC knocked down their 10 cups before we could hit more than six, and they ran over to their friends and began celebrating.

They didn't think we would be hitting those four cups to send the game into overtime, but we knew differently. The fact that they stepped away from the table as though the game were over was disrespectful enough to throw us into a rage of throwing fury. Without hesitation, my partner, Chauffeur, stepped up, threw fire, and burned one cup to the ground. I stepped up . . . fired . . . hit. Again it was Chauffeur's turn, and once again, with an awkward two-cup rack remaining, he drained it.

At that point I felt like I was shooting at an unmissable five-gallon bucket. The gently thrown 40-millimeter sphere sunk into the cup as if being pulled by some incredibly strong force, splashing beer over the sides and dousing the table in delicious droplets. No time to rest and celebrate our amazing comeback, though—overtime was to begin posthaste.

We could tell that hitting those four cups to send the game into OT shocked and drained the IWC. We quickly dispatched of our opponents in overtime, and both teams prepared for the second and final game of the match.

The other team was clearly winded, having spent most of their energy prematurely celebrating their victory. On the other hand, we were super-pumped, pissed, and ready to go. We knew we were going to throw the hell out of those Ping-Pong balls, and we did. We blew up the 10 cups before the IWC this time, putting the pressure on them to send it to overtime.

Stepping up, they hit some huge shots to make it to the last cup. On their last throw, though, there was hesitation—a big mistake. You just have to step up and fire. I was already celebrating in my mind when—after one last fondling of his crotch—our opponent shot. Bink! The ball hit the rim and bounced harmlessly to the floor.

And with that, the jumping around, falling, fist pounding, and blowing out of voices began, with no intention of stopping. The rush of emotions was insane, and we were lucky to have so many friends there to celebrate with and share the excitement. We knew this was the most important victory of our illustrious Beer Pong careers, and that we may never be in that position again. We didn't just win it for us, we won it for every one of our friends who played as adamantly as we did growing up, the ones that beat us and forced us to be better players, until finally, we became the best.

—Jeremy Hughes

Moms Gone Wild

When a parent arrives home to discover her son has thrown
a party, she reacts in an unexpected fashion.

We were at my friend's house for a fairly large gathering of people, not quite an out-of-control house party, but not a small get-together by any means. We were all in the basement, with Beer Pong in one of the main rooms and the movie *Beerfest* playing in the other. You could say beer was the main focus of this social gathering.

It got deeper and deeper into the night, and suddenly the mom of the kid whose house this was came home. We all panicked—the Beer Pong table was out, bottles and cans were everywhere, tons of cars were in the driveway and street, and strangers were littered throughout the house. Not something a parent wants to come home to.

The kid whose house it was went upstairs to talk to his mom, and next thing we knew, she came downstairs—but not to kick anyone out, yell at all of us, or say how much of a disappointment her son was. Instead, she came down to play some good old-fashioned Beer Pong versus her son's best friend.

We couldn't believe it—this was the funniest thing ever, especially since we thought we were all gonna get kicked out. Instead, we had a unique, highly entertaining game of Beer Pong to watch.

The game started, and everyone's eyes were fixated on the match at hand. With each ball tossed, people oohed and aahed as the ball missed for both sides.

The kid got off to a good start and knocked down a couple of the mom's cups. As expected, the game was looking one-sided. After all, the age gap was enormous. Plus, the mom was apparently out at the bars earlier, so her accuracy and Beer Pong abilities might have been a little worse than usual.

But the mom struck back, holding her own for the next few cups. The crowd started rooting for her. What could be better than this old lady humiliating a friend of theirs? It would be talked about for weeks.

But the kid wasn't wavering, either. Eventually, it was down to just one cup on both sides. The boy tossed and . . . missed! The mom tossed it up . . . miss. This went back and forth until suddenly the mom nailed it. The boy went for his rebuttal and . . . in and out. The mom had won!

I don't know what was going through the kid's head after this stunning, embarrassing loss, but it was probably something like, "Holy crap—I just lost at Beer Pong to my friend's 40-year-old mom!"

—*Paul J. Frank*

COACH SAYS

[Editor: The Coach has been rendered speechless by the shock of someone losing to their friend's mom.]

How to Be a
Beer Pong Photojournalist

They say a picture is worth a thousand words. Four of those words are, "Play," "More," "Beer," and "Pong." That's right: photos recruit more players.

The growth of the sport is dependent on growing its fan base. And although the stories you have just read help document the phenomenon, nothing grabs the populace more than a well-shot photograph. And there is no better way to grab more populaces than by distributing these images online.

But before you start clicking and posting, here are some important tips to improve your shutter skills:

DO compose like a pro. The No. I professional tip is to place your subject off-center for a more dynamic photo. Divide the frame into horizontal and vertical thirds. And place your primary subject near the intersections. The No. 2 tip is to shoot only attractive people.

DO capture the thrills of victory and the agonies of defeat. The raw, visceral highs and lows of the sport are much more compelling than how many cups you can stack in a rack. We're just saying.

DO capture the ball in midair. Nothing speaks to the sport's inherent drama like a ball about to enter the final cup, or an opponent's open mouth or exposed cleavage. But keep it real. You can tell a staged photo by the obvious fact that the other team is, well, nonexistent.

DON'T waste your time with improper lighting. If you are outside, late afternoon is a great time to shoot. If indoors, be aware that an on-camera flash doesn't work beyond seven feet away, so get close to your subjects. Note: Use a fill light if the searchlight from the cop car is shining directly on the subjects.

DON'T fill the frame with "That Guy." The world needs another shot of an over-served, sweaty guy or girl about to do a face plant like it needs another celebutante. There is so much more to the sport than Belushi antics. So keep it classy, San Diego.

DON'T show people posing with fake gang signs. There is nothing more discrediting to the sport than suburbanites mocking the plight of inner-city youth. If you are a gang member, though, please represent all you want.

Smashing Time

A top-ranked player reveals how he came
to make a career playing Beer Pong.

My name is Michael Popielarski, and this is the story of how I wound up on the Beer Pong circuit and made thousands of dollars along the way.

I'm from Long Island, New York, and I was introduced to Beer Pong at a house party. Some time later, a friend called me and asked me to play a Beer Pong tournament for money with him. We wound up placing second, losing to my future partner, Ron Hamilton (aka Mr. Automatic).

Some regular players in the bar started asking me to play because they thought I was good, and before long I was winning tournaments. Meanwhile, Ron and his partner won a satellite tournament for a free trip to the second World Series of Beer Pong (WSOBP). After playing him a few more times we started becoming friendly, and when his partner said he couldn't take off of work to play, I suggested to Ron that we play some tournaments together, and if all went well I could be his partner at the WSOBP in Vegas. As a well-known player and a veteran on the circuit, Ron would be taking a big risk on a rookie like me, but he said yes, and that's how our Beer Pong team, "Smashing Time," was formed.

We played together for about two weeks before the WSOBP and won a few tournaments. In Vegas, we went 12 and 0 in the preliminaries—good for a No. 1 ranking. Not too shabby for a team that formed two weeks before the biggest Beer Pong tournament of the year. We lost two bad games in the next round, though, and finished ranked ninth. But since we did so well overall, we decided to keep playing together.

In the two and a half years since our first WSOBP together, we've traveled around and played dozens of big tournaments. As of July '08, I'm ranked as the best player on the World Pong Tour circuit with 14 total wins, including three wins for spring break trips and seven wins for bids to the WSOBP IV (Smashing Time were WSOBP IV champions, winning $50,000!). At the WSOBP III we went 12 and 0 with a plus-54 cup differential in

OVERHEARD OVER
THE TABLE

••••••••••••••••

PointsInCase.com is a popular college humor Web site that features daily quotes from campuses around the country. Below are several tidbits that give a feeling for the back stories that players bring to every game of Beer Pong.

"Okay, Dad, you have to drink from that cup. Wait, you are supposed to take . . . Oh, okay, guys, game over. My dad just drank the ball."
— *Jeff, playing Beer Pong with his dad at Illinois State University*

Liz: "Oh my god, I think we wrote everything backwards."
Bekah: "Liz, were you standing in front of the mirror?"
Liz: "Oh crap."
— *Commenting on homemade T-shirts claiming they were the Beer Pong champs, SUNY Alfred*

"Man . . . I ain't never think throwing a ball into a cup could be so interesting."
— *Francis, shrewdly commenting on his first-ever game of Beer Pong, Cornell University*

Peter: "Dad is the best Beer Pong partner ever!"
Peter's mom: "Well, what about me?!"
Peter: "Uhhh . . . "
Peter's mom: "SCREW YOU PETER. SCREW YOU!"
— *The Clark family in a moment of crisis, Penn State University*

"First, we're going to need a flat table. Does anyone have a flat table?"
— *Jason, while reading the rules of Beer Pong*

the preliminaries, which ranked us No. 1 overall. Being the only team to ever go undefeated in the prelims two years in a row was a WSOBP record, and our plus-54 cup differential was another WSOBP record.

I credit a lot of my winning to having a 6-foot-6-inch frame that allows me to make a shorter shot across an eight-foot table than other players. I also think my athletic background in basketball and baseball helped me become a great Beer Pong player. A basketball foul shot is the same motion to me as a Beer Pong shot, and being a baseball player growing up gave me the depth perception and aim I needed. I play the game simple: I shoot all front cups to use my height to my advantage, and at the end of each game I shoot second to get the balls back or end the game completely.

I've had the good fortune of basically earning a yearly income from playing Beer Pong. In 2007, I earned more money playing Beer Pong than I did at my full-time job. I've also had the opportunity to travel to many states for events, and I'll be venturing to Jamaica and Mexico soon to play some of the top teams from around the world.

Amazingly, I've even been recognized at parties by some younger followers of the sport who have recognized me through websites and other places. It's kind of crazy looking back and thinking this sport I used to play for fun can turn people into a kind of celebrity with certain crowds. They say everyone finds their calling in life, and I guess this happens to be mine.

—*Michael Popielarski*

The Greatest Shot Ever Made

A dramatic shot puts an end to a marathon game of pong.

In a game of one-on-one Beer Pong, my friends Matt and Randy were in double OT. It was a heated contest, with tempers and skills both at their peak.

To defend himself from losing on a Chill Cup Rule, Randy stacked a cup on top of his chill cup (a foolproof method for foiling an opponent) and then proceeded to make one of his two shots.

Immediately after drinking a hit cup, Matt threw one ball at Randy's drinking cup—knocking off the stacked-cup shield—and then quickly threw a second ball, sinking it into Randy's chill cup and ending the game with a forced forfeiture.

All Randy could do was watch as Matt made two of the most memorable shots in the history of the game.

— *AJ Canonico*

COACH SAYS

The Chill Cup Rule is another name for the Sniper Rule, aka Death Cup, and means a shot made into an out-of-play cup being held in your opponent's hand is an instant victory. About as satisfying as winning a pool game on an eight-ball scratch. But we'll take it. Am I right, or am I right?

The Beer Pong Protégée

The battle of the sexes is never fiercer than when the only thing separating man from woman is a Beer Pong table and pride.

As a seasoned upperclassman, I introduced my doe-eyed friend, Ellen, to Beer Pong. At first I thought her incredible skill was just beginner's luck, but I now know that this girl is simply a natural.

One night we showed up at a house party when not much else was going on. We didn't know the people who lived there, but beer is beer, and we were on it. The party was completely lame, so naturally we began suggesting that someone set up Beer Pong. After a bit, we were in full swing and playing the guy who owned the house. So we set up the table for him and his partner, and immediately he was trying to change the rules. I vocalized my unhappiness with his "ghetto-ass rules."

In retrospect, I was a mouthy girl—someone he didn't know and who was drinking his beer. But this didn't cross my mind at the time, of course. So I continued to insist—loudly—that we were gonna kick his ass, even *with* his shady rules.

Long story short: We were down to one cup each, and he sank the shot first, and even though he tried to stop us from getting our rebuttal shot, everyone in the room disagreed. So we took our final shot. And I hit it. Thus we went into triple-cup overtime, and I started making jokes about him losing to girls.

On our last shot, quiet Ellen made the proclamation, "Mary, I can't even see the f-ing cups." The crowd hushed. But with a dramatic spin, she turned around and proceeded to sink the winning shot. We flashed him a smile and a "told you so," and he was fuming.

One thing led to another, and I'm proud to say that is the one and only time I've ever been physically thrown out of a party.

—*Elizabeth S.*

Mismatched Matchup

If you think you've had some bad Beer Pong partners, check out this tale from a guy who was paired with a true academic.

About two years ago, I went to some dude's house for a little get-together. As soon as I entered the door, some of my buddies insisted that we start some good ole Beer Pong. My friends, being the pricks that they are, teamed up with each other, leaving me with no partner. So I started to search for a teammate.

The games were about to start, so the guy that owned the house teamed me up with someone: his philosophy professor. The prof had come for the party but didn't want to imbibe, so I had to drink all the sunk cups. To top that off, it was his first time playing, and we got caught playing the two best players there.

The game started, and Mr. Philosophy missed. I hit my cup. The other team played, and only one of them hit their cup.

Our turn. The teacher missed, and I hit the cup.

This went on and on until there was only one cup left on each side. It was our turn, and the prof missed, as usual. About 20 people were around the table taunting the opposing team, waiting to see if I could make six in a row and beat the top team despite my hapless professorial partner.

I called for quiet. The room silenced. You could feel the tension in the air. I nailed the shot, the crowd went wild, and the other team missed both their rebuttals.

I won the game single-handedly, and now every time I go to parties, the amazing match always seems to pop up in conversation.

— *Matthew B.*

WANT MORE STORIES?

This tale is one of over 4,000 literary masterpieces in the annals of CollegeStories.com. And for the ultimate canon of campus antics, check out the book *Class Dismissed: 75 Outrageous, Mind-Expanding College Exploits (and Lessons That Won't Be on the Final)*.

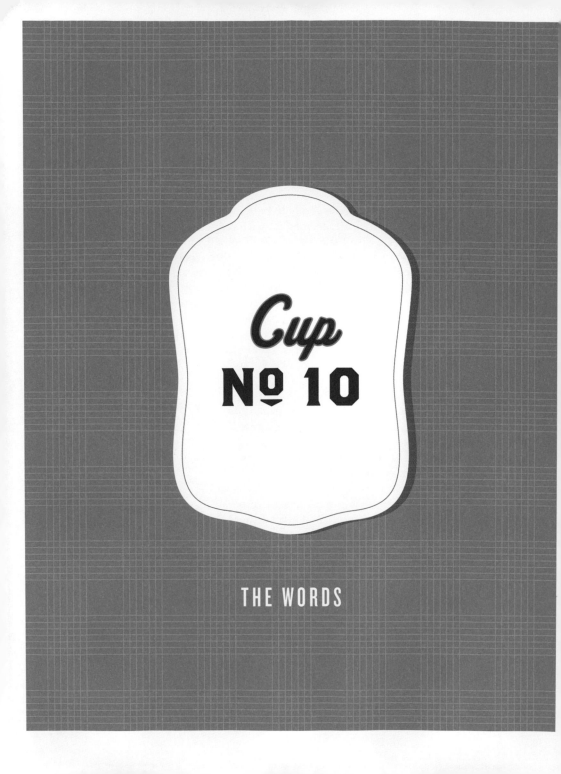

Cup

№ 10

THE WORDS

BEFORE YOU CAN PLAY LIKE A CHAMP, YOU NEED TO TALK LIKE A CHAMP.

TO UNDERSTAND THIS UNIQUE SPORT, one must first understand the building blocks of its experience. And those are cups, balls, and beer. But after that foundation comes the game's unique language.

As all fans know, you can tell a lot about a sport through the words used to convey it. Legendary comedian George Carlin famously compared the language of two American sporting institutions:

Football is concerned with downs. "What down is it?"

Baseball is concerned with ups. "Who's up? Are you up? I'm not up! He's up!"

Football has hitting, clipping, spearing, piling on, personal fouls, late hitting, and unnecessary roughness.

Baseball has the sacrifice.

In other words, the differences in the culture of each sport are worn quite clearly on their semantic sleeves.

As someone who is reading this book, you obviously possess a desire to understand what makes the game tick—to get a taste of this sport of champions. So to facilitate this, we've compiled the following glossary of the most common and important terms in the ever-expanding Beer Pong lexicon.

3-RACK

n. A cup rack configured 2-1.

5-RACK

n. A cup rack configured 3-2.

6-RACK

n. A cup rack configured 3-2-1.

10-RACK

n. A cup rack configured 4-3-2-1.

12-RACK

n. Dual cup racks configured 3-2-1.

AIR BALL

n. A shot attempt that clears the table without hitting a surface—much less a cup.

ARC

n. The path the ball follows from the moment it leaves your hand until it reaches the cup.

ARRANGEMENT

n. Any configuration of cups in a rack.

AZTEC

See *5-Rack.*

BABY-BACK

n. A one-ball bring-back. Does not involve eating ribs or listening to Sir Mix-A-Lot.

BALL

n. An object used to throw into cups, usually a 40-millimeter table-tennis ball.

BAR SCAR

n. The ink from a hand stamp applied at the bar you played at the previous night.

> **EXAMPLE:** "Before you go for a job interview, it's best to wash off any *bar scars.*"

BEER

n. A beverage produced by a brewing process based on the fermentation of starches derived from some cereals. The liquid of choice for Beer Pong.

BEER PONG

n. A sport that involves players at opposite ends of a table throwing a table-tennis ball across the table with the intent of landing the ball in a formation of cups set up across from them at the opposite end of the table. Return to beginning of this book for more information.

BEER SCOOTER

n. The safest way of returning from a night of Beer Pong. Also known as "walking" and "two feet and a heartbeat."

> EXAMPLE: "After losing so many games in a row, I left my car at Barry's and just took the old *beer scooter* home."

BEERACLE

n. A miracle that is caused by almighty beer, e.g., making 10 straight cups in a game.

BEIRUT

n. An old-school name for Beer Pong that dates back to the "Great Optimization," when the table-tennis paddles were first dispensed with.

BEVERAGE

n. Any liquid used to fill a cup. See *beer.*

BLING

See *wash cup.*

BLOCK

v. To attempt to swat, smack, or grab a shot once it hits a surface. May result in unforeseen or undesirable consequences when attempted by an overly belligerent player.

BLOW

v. To produce air from one's mouth and direct it downward into the cup in a defensive effort to push out a ball that is spinning around the rim or inner walls of the cup.

BLUNTED

1. *adj.* Shut out of a game.
2. *adj.* So dirty that it needs to get discarded, as in a ball or cup.

> EXAMPLE: "Get that nasty thing out of here. That ball is *blunted*!"

BOLT

v. To down a beverage in one sip.

> EXAMPLE: "After all that smack you talked, you'd better *bolt* that cup, Barry."

BOUNCE

n. Any attempt to intentionally bounce a ball off the table into a cup. Typically results in removal of two cups if successful. However, once the ball hits the table, it can be blocked.

BRACKET

n. A system used in tournaments to determine match winners, losers, and progression toward a final winner.

BREAKING THE SEAL

v. To perform the first urination of the night. Can lead to in-game distractions if not properly managed.

> EXAMPLE: "We're just getting started, and you're already *breaking the seal*? I don't want to wait for your ass when you have to go again in 10 minutes."

BIG DICK

n. A re-rack that involves three cups arranged in a line back to front.

BITCH CUP

n. The absolute middle cup in a 10-rack; the easiest cup to hit.

BRING-BACK

n. A game rule that requires the balls be returned to the shooter when both shot attempts are made in one turn.

BUMP OFF

v. To beat one's opponents by only one cup.

> EXAMPLE: "We barely got *bumped off* by those lucky chuckers."

CALLED SHOT

n. A sunk cup that the player actually announces before shooting.

CHILL CUP

n. A cup used by a player to hold an additional beverage that's not part of the rack of in-play cups.

> EXAMPLE: "Dude, don't drink from the rack cups. Pour it into a *chill cup* first."

CHUCKER

See *rack shooter.*

COBE

n. Abbreviation for "confirmation of ball entry," a visual image of the ball inside a cup. In trick-shot videos, it's considered the all-important "money shot" after an impressive throw.

> EXAMPLE: "I almost thought he actually knocked down that shot from 40 feet away with his eyes closed, until I realized they had never shown the *COBE*."

COLLATERAL CUP

n. A cup that is unintentionally sunk either from a ricochet or missed throw.

CONSOLIDATE

See *re-rack.*

CUP

n. A drinking container typically made from plastic.

CUP MARGIN

n. The apparent size of the rim of a cup. Can fluctuate depending on angle of shot and number of beers imbibed.

DEAD BALL

n. A ball that is out of play.

DEAD CUP

n. A cup that is out of play.

COACH SAYS

Bring-backs are the Beer Pong gods' way of rewarding the strong and punishing the weak. You gotta love that.

DEATH CUP
See *sniper rule.*

DEFENSE
n. Any attempt to distract an opponent or block a shot.

DIAMOND
n. A four-cup rack

DICK
n. A re-rack that involves two cups arranged back to front.

DICK 'EM
v. See *dick.*

DICK RIDER
n. A player who mimics the style of his opponent and hits only the cups his opponent hits.

DIESEL
n. A non-light beer.
EXAMPLE: "After downing seven slices of pizza and five pieces of fried chicken at the all-you-can-eat buffet, Dirk had no desire to play with *diesels.*"

DISTRACTION
n. The diversion of a shooter's attention from the cup.

DOGGY STYLE
adj. See *dick.*

DOUBLE UP
v. To have both players on a team sink two cups in a single turn. Typically results in a *bring-back.*

DOUBLE-TAP
v. To hit the last cup twice to end the game with no rebuttals.

DRIFTER
n. A cup that mysteriously moves out of position on its own due to a tilted, slippery, or wet surface.
EXAMPLE: "The players were initially alarmed when the *drifter* moved a good three inches to the left."

DROPPIN' BOMBS
See *on fire.*

DUNCE CUPS
n. The back corner cups of a rack.

BEER PONG FACTOID

In Game 3 of the 1932 World Series, Babe Ruth belted his famous "called shot" home run, his last career hit in postseason play. It is also a little-known fact that the Bambino would shoot a mean game of Pong if he was still around.

ELBOW RULE

n. A common rule that requires a shooter to keep his/her elbow behind the edge of the table for a shot to be valid.

END OF GAME

n. Sinking of the last cup. Typically accompanied by, but not limited to, whooping for joy, chest bumping, talking smack, letting loose a stream of invectives, weeping in the corner, or staring deep into space.

EYE-TO-EYE

See *snake eyes.*

FINAL CUP

n. The last cup left in a rack, which once hit, ends the game.

FINGERING

n. The act of using one's finger to flick out a ball spinning around the rim in the name of defense.

FIRE

See *on fire.*

FISH

n. A Beer Pong novice.
> **EXAMPLE:** "I'd like to throttle that idiot *fish* who just caught my shot in midair."

FLIPPER

n. A player who flips the table after a loss or when the party is over.

FORMATION

n. Any arrangement of cups that are touching.

FULL CONTACT

n. A game of Beer Pong that involves full body contact to retrieve loose balls. Known to prompt colleges students and sloth-like adults into two rare activities: showering and doing laundry.

GENTLEMAN'S RULE

n. A dictate stating that in overtime, each player shoots until he misses. Has no relation to the social or economic standing of the players involved.

GOAL-TENDING

n. Blocking of a live ball. Results in a one-cup penalty.

BEER PONG FACTOID

Anthony Edwards, who played Tom Cruise's loyal friend Nick "Goose" Bradshaw in *Top Gun,* made one of his first film appearances as Stoner Bud in *Fast Times at Ridgemont High.* And people who like *Fast Times* often play Beer Pong.

GOOSE
1. *n.* A good partner.
2. *n.* The shape your hand and arm make when using serious follow-through.

GRABBING
n. An attempt to catch a ball that has hit a surface in order to block it.

GRIP
n. The technique of holding the ball. Sometimes used to create spin, flummox an opponent, or entertain oneself during a lopsided match.

HEAD CUP
n. The front cup of a rack.

HIT
See *sink*.

HOOVER
v. To drink a spilled beer from whatever surface it's on—regardless of sanitation concerns. Often the job of the spiller.
> EXAMPLE: "After Karl spilled a full rack of Beast all of over the floor, you should have seen him *Hoover* it up."

HOUSE RULES
n. Any rules established prior to a match that are unorthodox or not obvious.
> EXAMPLE: "Did you hear about this guy's bizarre *house rules* involving Mad Dog in the head cup?"

HUNG-OVER
adj. Exhibiting excessive leaning while shooting. Not to be confused with being hungover from exorbitant drinking.
> EXAMPLE: "Look at the way he's throwing—that guy is really *hung-over*."

ICE
See *diamond*.

KARL
See *final cup*.

KNOCK-OVER
n. A cup that tips or falls when hit by the ball or a player.

LARRY
1. *n.* A beer that has been opened but not fully consumed. See also *wounded soldier*.
2. *n.* A player who does not drink his sunk cups.

COACH SAYS

If leaning is allowed, take full advantage of the situation. If not, step back and respect the line!

LAST CUP
See *final cup*.

LEANER
n. A player who intentionally crosses the plane when shooting. Also known as a cheater and a stink.

LET IT RIDE
n. A type of match in which players are not allowed to interfere with a ball's chance of hitting a cup. In other words, no defense until it's obvious the ball has no chance of being sunk.

LEVEL RACK
See *on the level*.

LIGHTS OUT
See *on fire*.

LIST
n. A piece of paper or a dry-erase board that's used to list the on-deck teams in order of turn. Considered as sacred a document as the original Declaration of Independence.

LIST JUMPER(S)
n. A player or team that attempts to play as soon as possible by doctoring the list.

LIVE BALL
n. A ball that's been shot and has not yet touched any surface or cup.

LIVE CUP
n. Any cup that's still in play and needs to be sunk before it can be removed.
> EXAMPLE: "Don't touch that! It's a *live cup*."

LONE WOLF
n. The last cup remaining on a table, or any solitary cup.
> EXAMPLE: "That *lone wolf* was the beginning of my downfall that night. I couldn't sink it for anything."

LOOSE RACK
n. A rack that has been set up poorly, resulting in lopsided cups and uneven spacing.

LUCK SHOT
n. A shot that either bounces or rims out of one cup and into a different cup.

MID-RACK
n. A re-rack that occurs between a team's two shot attempts. Some rule variations do not allow mid-racks.

MISS
n. A shot attempt that does not sink a cup. Often accompanied by a loud sigh, angry gesture, or obscenity.

MONEY CUP

1. *n.* The last cup, or any designated cup that's worth cash used in a betting game.

2. *n.* A cup full of a game beverage or a potent combination of something else.

MONEY GAME

n. Any match that involves a bet or money. Has been known to convert the closest of friends into hated adversaries.

ON DECK

adj. Being the next team to play. On-deck players often hover annoyingly near the table rather than in an assigned circle as in baseball.

ON FIRE

adj. Describing a player who has sunk three cups or more in a row.

ON THE LEVEL

adj. Describing a rack that has been set up perfectly—tight, with even fills and no loose or lopsided cups.

>   **EXAMPLE:** "Quit your bitching, Barry, that rack is *on the level!*"

ONE-TWO

n. Hitting the last two cups in a row to end the game.

ORPHAN CUP

See *drifter.*

OVERTIME

n. The extra playing period that ensues if a team successfully hits all the cups in their rebuttal.

PADDLE

n. An ancient tool designed specifically to hit a Ping-Pong ball. Variants include a fraternity version built to smack pledges on their bare hindquarters.

PENALTY

n. Any act that incurs the removal of a cup.

PERFECT GAME

n. A game in which all the cups in a rack are hit without any misses.

PHANTOM CUP

n. A spot where a cup once stood but now has been removed. Usually invoked when a player's shots repeatedly fall in this location.

>   **EXAMPLE:** "We lost because I kept hitting the *phantom cup* like it was my job."

COACH SAYS

There have been only 17 perfect games thrown in major league baseball history, which tells me that maybe baseball players aren't such good athletes after all.

PITCHER
n. A large container with a handle and lip used to hold and pour large amounts of liquid to fill a rack. Prevents griping and needless game delays.

PLANE
n. The invisible area that should not be crossed when attempting a shot. Venturing into this forbidden zone may subject a player to taunting and/or mockery.

PLAYER
n. Any person who is a legal shooter, regardless of whether or not they have any game.

POOL PONG
n. Beer Pong played on a raft in a pool.

PREGAME
v. To party before heading out to the main party event. Often includes a warm-up game of Beer Pong. Often used as *pre* for short.

PRE-PARTY
See *pregame.*

PYRAMID
n. Any arrangement of cups that makes a perfect triangle, e.g., 10-rack, 6-rack, 3-rack.

RACK
n. Any arrangement of cups used to play a match.

RACK SHOOTER
n. A player who makes only lucky shots but never aims, often the envy of those on a cold shooting streak.

REARRANGE
See *re-rack.*

REBUTTAL
n. An opportunity to take one final round of shots after all of a team's cups have been hit. If said team hits all of the opponent's remaining cups in turn, the game is tied and overtime ensues.

REDEMPTION
See *rebuttal.*

REFORMATION
See *re-rack.*

REMOVAL
v. The act of taking a sunk cup out of the rack, usually done quickly and inconspicuously so as to barely acknowledge the other team's success. Usually precedes consumption of said cup's contents.

RE-RACK
v. To rearrange the formation of cups to create a new rack.

RETURN
See *bring-back.*

RIM

n. The top and outer part of the opening of a cup. According to some players, the location of 99 percent of their missed shots.

  EXAMPLE: "That loss was just plain bad luck—the last 15 of my shots hit *rim*."

RIM JOB

See *rim-out*.

RIM-OUT

n. A shot that enters a cup but spins out, resulting in a miss.

RINGER

n. A player who is recruited for a team because of his/her skills.

RINSE CUP

See *wash cup*.

ROLL-BACK

See *bring-back*.

'RUIT

Short for *Beirut*.

SET UP/SETUP

1. *v.* To arrange the cups in a rack and fill them with a beverage at the beginning of a match. Often done by the losing or challenging team as a form of pregame humiliation.
2. *n.* An arrangement of cups.

SHA-DIAMOND

See *diamond*.

SHOOTER

n. A player with possession of the ball who can legally attempt a shot. Does not include random spectators who amuse themselves by throwing wayward balls at cups in play.

SHOOTING ANGLE

n. The direction of your stance in relation to the cups.

SHOOTING AREA/SHOOTING LINE

See *plane*.

SHOOTING ORDER

n. The proper order in which a player can shoot—two balls per team per turn.

COACH SAYS

To paraphrase Vince Lombardi, Beer Pong is like life—it requires perseverance, self-denial, hard work, sacrifice, dedication, and respect for authority. But even if you don't possess any of these attributes, you'll still enjoy playing.

THE "EYES" HAVE IT

....

Other meanings for the phrase snake eyes:

1. A roll of dice that results in two I's, the probability of which is 1:36, or 2.7 percent.
2. A member of the G.I. Joe team and a full-fledged ninja master.
3. A 1998 thriller starring Nicholas Cage that grossed a middling $55 million.
4. The actual eyes of a snake, which are covered by clear scales rather than movable eyelids—thus leaving the eyes in a perpetually open position.

SHOT

n. Any attempt to project the ball toward a rack with the intent of sinking a cup.

SHUTOUT

n. A game in which the losing team does not sink any cups. Often results in depression and a lengthy hiatus from the sport.

SINK

v. To land the ball in a cup, resulting in removal of that cup.

SINKAGE RATE

n. The percentage of shots made, calculated by dividing shots made by shots attempted.

EXAMPLE: "With a *sinkage rate* of 80 percent, Krazee-Eyez Killa was unstoppable in the championship game."

SLUMP BUSTER

n. A cakewalk game played to recharge a team after a series of demoralizing losses.

EXAMPLE: "Rather than sitting in the corner stewing and muttering to himself, he decided to line up a *slump buster* to improve his spirits."

SNAKE EYES

n. A method used to determine possession prior to the start of a match in which opposing players stare each other in the eyes and simultaneously shoot the ball at the rack.

SNIPER RULE

n. Game variation in which intentionally sinking an opposing player's chill cup results in an automatic win.

SORBO

See *flipper.*

SPELUNK

v. To sink a cup without hitting anything but beer. Similar to a "swoosh" in basketball.

SPLIT

n. An arrangement of cups that have a space between them.

STRAY CUP
See *drifter.*

STREET KNUCKLER
n. A player who got beat early and is angling for another match. Street knucklers typically try to weasel their way to the top of the list by any means necessary and have been known to frequently switch partners.

STRIP PONG
n. A version of Beer Pong that involves the removal of clothing as shots are sunk.
> EXAMPLE: "I hope that video of me in my tighty-whiteys playing *strip pong* doesn't make its way onto YouTube."

SUDDEN DEATH
n. A match that involves no rebuttals, resulting in an ending so abrupt and shocking as to create a state of near-cardiac arrest in the losing players.

SUPER DICK
n. A re-rack in which four cups are arranged in a line back to front.

SWATTING
v. An attempt to hit or smack a ball once it has touched a surface in order to block it.

SWEET BABY RAY
n. Two bring-backs in a row at the beginning of a match, resulting in a six-cup re-rack prior to your opponent's first shot attempt.

TABLE
n. Any surface used to play a match. Typically a Ping-Pong table or another table with similar dimensions that can withstand frequent beer spillage and assorted other adverse conditions.

TEAM
n. A combination of two players who are legal shooters in a match and may or may not like one another.

THROW
See *shot.*

THROWING PATTERN
See *shooting order.*

TORPEDO
n. A player who rarely misses a cup.
> EXAMPLE: "Watch out, that guy on Team Ramrod is a *torpedo*—he sinks everything."

TRIANGLE
n. Any configuration of cups that makes a perfect triangle.

TRE
See *3-rack.*

TRE BOMB
n. An instance of hitting the last three cups in a row to end the match.

UPB

n. Abbreviation for "unidentified pong bruise." These mild injuries appear the day after playing with no direct cause— or at least no memory of the cause.

> **EXAMPLE:** "I didn't think that the game got out of hand, but I woke up with *UPBs* across my butt and some girl's number in my pocket."

WARM-UP RACK

n. The first re-rack of a match.

WASH CUP

n. A cup, usually filled with water, used to rinse off dirty balls.

WATER CUP

See *wash cup*.

WOUNDED SOLDIER

n. An unfinished beer. See also *Larry*.

> **EXAMPLE:** "Can you believe those guys—they left three *wounded soldiers* on the table and fled the scene without saying a word."

WET

1. *adj.* Sunk, as a ball in a cup.
2. *adj.* Really good, used in reference to Beer Pong player.

> **EXAMPLE:** "Be careful, that guy is *wet*. He can't miss."

ZAMBONI

n. Anything that can be used to clean up the table. Preferably a rag or a roll of paper towels.

> **EXAMPLE:** "Quick, get the *Zamboni* before that spillage stains my hardwood floor!"

The New Sports Idioms on the Culture Block

There is no clearer example of a sport's indoctrination into popular culture than when its vocabulary becomes part of the general lexicon. Traditional sports have had a **head start** (from horse racing) in becoming idiomatic **heavyweights** (from boxing).

Since Beer Pong is a sport befitting of the same stature in our culture, we'd like to suggest the following new sports idioms. Please review the following examples, and try to incorporate these expressions in conversation at least once a day.

*"We got off to a bad start last night. I'm sorry about what I said about your mom. Can we just **dip it in the wash cup** and start all over again?"*

*"I'm not sure if she's out of the closet, but there are rumors that she **shoots from the other side of the table**."*

*"In Of Mice and Men, Lennie Small was not physically diminutive as his name alludes, but mentally he was clearly **not playing with a tight rack**."*

*"Ladies and gentlemen of the jury, my client could have in no way committed the crime. Now his fate rests on your decision today—**the ball is now in your cup**."*

*"The brinksmanship of the Cuban Missile Crisis escalated the last two superpowers to the point of being just **one cup** away from all-out nuclear war."*

Acknowledgments

CONTRIBUTORS OF BEER PONG GREATNESS:

Peter Altholtz, Michael Balkman, Chris Barish, Mark Berry, Joey Danelo, Jere Daniell, Paul J. Frank, Aaron Heffner, Steve Hofstetter, Jason Hughes, Jeremy Hughes, Neil Guerriero, Austin Lanham, Tim Mentink, Amber Morales, Ben Morrissey, Ryan Murphy, Mark Musco, Rick Odom, Michael Popielarski, Ronny Rader, Peter Rusch, Nicholas Velissaris, Court Sullivan, Eric Welch and The Hilltoppers—Andrew Boyle, Gabe Rivera, Dean Wright, and The CT All-Stars—John Bustelos, Michael Carbrey, Bill Gula, Bush Lydon, Porter McKinnon, Michael Parent, Aaron Pawluk, Jeremy Peck, Tony Pontbriand, and Adam Rogers.

The authors would like to raise a cup to the entire team at Chronicle Books, especially Emily Haynes, Sarah Malarkey, Jennifer Kong, Andrew Schapiro, Becca Cohen, and for a brief moment, Matt Robinson; to our friends at Levine Greenberg, especially Stephanie Kip Rostan and Monika Verma; and to all the players of Beer Pong the world over.

Ben would like to personally thank Ryan "Atlanta's Movie Examiner" McNally and Michael "Check out *Assault on the Senses*" Ferrari for their editorial acumen; Derrick Pittman for pouring the foundation; all the Moon Pi's of WFU for many a game in Taylor House; and especially Valerie and Gillian for always supporting my absurd pursuits.

Dan would like to personally thank Jenny, the first lady of Beer Pong, for being the best partner any player could ask for; all the CT All-Stars for being great friends and teammates; the Jefferson-Colt Posse and FC Burn for teaching me the sport; and the entire crew at GetBombed.com for helping make this all a reality.

ABOUT THE AUTHORS

BEN APPLEBAUM is an advertising creative director. As a co-founder of CollegeStories.com, he has written seriously about stupid stuff, including co-authoring *Turd Ferguson & The Sausage Party: An Uncensored Guide to College Slang* and *Class Dismissed: 75 Outrageous, Mind-Expanding, College Exploits*. He got his first taste of Beer Pong during his college days at Wake Forest University. Today he lives in Connecticut with his very tolerant wife and daughter.

DAN DISORBO is the mild-mannered art director and illustrator at PB&J Design, Inc., by day. But by night, he is the advocate and proprietor of all things Beer Pong, and co-founder of BOMBED Beer Pong and the Web site GetBombed.com. He honed his diverse skill set at the University of Connecticut and now lives in Connecticut with his beautiful wife and plenty of (beer pong) balls.

VISIT OUR APPROPRIATELY NAMED WEB SITE
WWW.THEBOOKOFBEERPONG.COM